# The Finishing Touch

## BOOKS BY BRUCE BLIVEN, JR.

*The Wonderful Writing Machine; Battle for Manhattan; Under the Guns: New York 1775–1776; Book Traveller; Volunteers, One and All; The Finishing Touch*

FOR CHILDREN: *The Story of D-Day: June 6, 1944; The American Revolution; From Pearl Harbor to Okinawa; From Casablanca to Berlin; New York: The Story of the World's Most Exciting City* (with Naomi Bliven)

# The
# Finishing Touch

### BRUCE BLIVEN, JR.
*Illustrated with photographs*

DODD, MEAD, & COMPANY, NEW YORK

Copyright © 1946, 1949, 1953, 1957, 1972, 1973,
   1974, 1976, 1978 by Bruce Bliven, Jr.
Printed in the United States of America
by The Haddon Craftsmen, Inc., Scranton, Penna.


1    2    3    4    5    6    7    8    9    10


Library of Congress Cataloging in Publication Data

Bliven, Bruce, date
   The finishing touch.

   1. United States—Biography. I. Title.
CT220.B53    920'.073    78–1356
ISBN 0–396–07534–7

*For William Shawn*

# Contents

# CHAPTER 1

# Introduction

THIS is a book about five perfectionists—
an author, an athlete, a mechanic, a salesman, and a
scientist—who resemble each other in more ways than
I realized when, over a period of twenty-five years, I
thought of them as magazine article subjects. In every
case, my attention was attracted to what my five subjects did, not who they were. I thought their occupa-
tional specialties were intriguing, unusual, and enter-
taining, and as I wrote outlines and talked to editors,
trying to get assignments to write the articles, those
were the values I tried to stress. My five subjects were
excuses to write about their work, and not about them
as celebrities. In the case of Dick Miles, the table-
tennis champion, my assignment was to write about
the table-tennis champion whoever he was, assuming
there was one. If, at the time, another man had held
the title, he would have been my subject.

Margaret Wise Brown was a friend of mine before

I began interviewing her for a *Life* "Close-Up," but she had not previously explained to me the seriousness with which she approached writing for very young children. In fact, she had always gone to considerable trouble to pretend that her writing was a splendid game, an elaborate joke or put-on to fool publishers, editors, educational ideologues, and librarians. Margaret pretended astonishment when I counted the number of books she had published between 1937 and 1947 and arrived at the total of fifty-three. I was not certain whether she was surprised by the number or by the idea that anyone would make a list and count the titles. Before Margaret died, in 1952, she had written another fifty books—her productivity was increasing —and had also composed the lyrics for twenty-one children's phonograph records, drawing, in nearly every case, on her own material that had already appeared in picture-book form. I liked Margaret's picture books in 1947, but I did not dream that she was producing classics. Half of all her books are in print in 1978, and I will not be surprised if the number grows.

The perfectionist side of Dick Miles's personality was no easier to perceive than Margaret Wise Brown's. When I first met Miles, he had won the United States Men's Singles table-tennis championship only twice, in 1945 and 1946. He wore his crown, or crowns, very lightly, and he was proud of the extraordinarily fast circular forehand he had invented, but he spoke so casually about his game that it took me a long time to appreciate how thoughtfully he had analyzed it and had worked at incorporating his insights into table-tennis form into the way he played the game. (I began by giving too much credit to the speed of his very speedy reflexes.) The clue to the way Miles had won at nineteen and was going on to dominate the American table-tennis scene throughout the fifties was best revealed by the way he talked about many other things —music, high-fidelity recordings, chess, poker. He was, and is, fascinated—whatever the field—by defining the best as well as deciding, analytically, what makes the difference between excellent and nonpareil.

It was Miles who gave me the idea of writing about William Hupfer, the piano-tone regulator and Hupfer's workshop in the basement of Steinway Hall on West Fifty-seventh Street. Miles had heard about Hupfer, and Hupfer's refined technical specialty, from one of the many musicians who are interested, by some mysterious chemistry, in table tennis. (I think it was Miles's pianist friend, Bernard Baslow, with whom Miles was swapping lessons.) Since perfect piano tone —that is, Steinway piano tone, as Hupfer identified it —was a considerable part of the idea of the piece, I did not have to search for the theme of Hupfer as a perfectionist. In any case, Hupfer at his workbench, cajoling the felts of a concert grand into prime condition, was the epitome of a craftsman at work—dignified, dedicated, and absolutely assured in every one of his movements. I doubt that he had ever been interviewed before. Certainly he had never been asked to explain what he did in so much detail by anyone except another piano mechanic. Hupfer seemed to enjoy my interminable questions, and luckily I was reporting the piece for *The New Yorker*, which made me feel that if I could learn *everything* about tone regulating, that would not be too much. William Shawn, the editor of the magazine, had given me the go-ahead, and, in talking about what I hoped to do, I had warned him that, along the way, I intended to describe the techniques of tone regulation in minute detail. Shawn had immediately said, "Oh, yes," and made me feel that such a description was an essential part of my project. So it did not cross my mind, nor has it since, that the technical details of the fine points of tone regulating may not be everyone's idea of an enthralling topic.

For years I kept an Idea File. It looked like a cooking recipe file on eight-by-five cards, because that is what it had been, originally. The idea of accompanying a book salesman on the road and describing the trials of his trade had been nesting in that file for a long time. I had not proposed it to an editor because I could not figure out how to find the right salesman. I wasn't thinking of superlatives, so he would not have to be the most successful book salesman in the country, and I was not worried about finding an average, or typical, book salesman, either. But I thought I would need to find an experienced traveller who knew just what he was doing, and could explain it to me with some style. Then I needed to find a salesman who would not mind taking me with him, and, in my imagination, this posed a great difficulty. How could a reporter sit in on a conversation between a book seller and a book buyer without being terribly in the way? I was afraid it was not possible.

George F. Scheer appeared before me as if by magic at a meeting of the Society of American Historians, as I mention in Chapter V. The "Book Salesman" card in my Idea File immediately popped into my mind— I had not thought about it for a long time—and the fact that Scheer was simultaneously engaged in several other occupations, too, struck me as an advantage, not a disqualification. Not long afterwards, Scheer and I had lunch together, and I felt certain, before the en-

tree had been served, that I had the right man. He
thought it would be all right if I travelled with him for
a while, although he warned me that since I had written some books, the experience might break my heart.
I told Scheer that I did not see how I could fail to get
in his and his buyers' way, even if I kept my mouth
tightly shut. Scheer laughed. "I can assure you," he
said, "that after the first moment or two, my buyers are
not even going to be aware that you are sitting there.
You don't realize how intense a selling session is, or
how hard we both work. My buyers will be too busy to
pay any attention to you, and so will I." Which was just
the way it worked out. Since Scheer is a logical, practical man, he knows that publishing is, and will remain,
an imperfect enterprise. Still, I define him as a perfectionist because he is not going to *accept* that fact, even
though he acknowledges it.

Everyone who has worked with Professor Cyril M.
Harris—students, academic colleagues, editors, con-
tributors to the books he has edited, architects, construction workers, the clients who have consulted him
about a variety of acoustic problems—has noticed
quickly that Harris is driven to get things exactly right.
It is his most obvious characteristic. For thirty years or
more Harris has wanted to build a perfect concert hall
*and* to convince the world that "perfect" is an imperfect word to describe the highest obtainable degree of
acoustic excellence. But his passion for the best ex-
tends to everything that interests him at all, including
musical performances and Cape Cod clam pie. He is,
by necessity, a crusader for the optimum, because his
work involves large groups of people. When Harris
agrees to act as acoustical consultant, he has to persuade his associates, who may be strangers, that the

success of the enterprise will depend on their becoming perfectionists, too. He seems to enjoy this aspect of teaching, like everything he does, but I suspect that he often finds it hard. When things go wrong—it is impossible to build anything as complex as a concert hall without some mishaps—Harris's solutions may cost the client tens of thousands of dollars more than he or she wanted to spend. No one except Harris exactly understands why a *slightly* less expensive correction won't do, and I am sure that Harris does not enjoy insisting, for the acoustics' sake, that the money be spent.

Nearly all my chapter on Harris, describing how he and Philip Johnson and John Burgee rebuilt Avery Fisher Hall, the home of the New York Philharmonic, during the summer of 1976, appeared in *The New Yorker* a couple of weeks (November 8, 1976) after the opening concert. Some of the biographical material about Harris's early life and early research is from a *New Yorker* Profile of Harris that had run only a little more than four years earlier, in the issue of June 17, 1972. The Profile was as much about New York City noise as it was about Harris. (Mayor Lindsay's administration, with considerable fanfare, was rewriting the City's noise-control code at the time, and Harris was almost certain, in advance, that the new law wouldn't work. As usual, Harris was right.) Still the fact that *The New Yorker* had already run my Profile of Harris inhibited me from suggesting a second long piece about Harris—or, at least, a long piece with Harris in the major role. (The magazine has no rule about writing about a person more than once; it was just that the interval seemed short.) I therefore proposed to Shawn, about a year in advance, that I do a *short* piece about the rebuilding for The Talk of the Town when the reconstruction was about complete. "Good," said Shawn.

A couple of months later, Shawn spoke to me about it. "I've been thinking about that Cyril Harris story," he said. "I think what we want is not a Talk story, but a full-sized article. Don't worry about the length." I was delighted, of course. "And about your feeling that it hasn't been very long since the Harris Profile. I've been thinking about *that,* too. I think the answer is that the two pieces are not at all alike. They are entirely different. And it just *happens* that Harris is the main character in them both." I mention this only because there is a sixth perfectionist not far behind the scenes in the larger part of this book, and his name is William Shawn.

Harris is frequently told by materials manufacturers that he is old-fashioned in his fondness for wood. They say that their products can do anything wood does, and do it better, and at less cost. "I am sure you are right," Harris replies, "but how many years has your product been tested in actual use? I am thinking about fifty years from now, and I know that wood will be as good then as it is now."

I am delighted by the way Harris turns the tables. He does not defend the traditional; he transforms it into a material for the future. He does not criticize the new, but only wonders what the test of time will show. Craftsmanship itself sometimes has seemed like misplaced emphasis, or outmoded. I have a hunch, on the contrary, that it is going to be even more highly valued than in the past.

My subjects are all extravagant in the sense that they never seem to know where or when they ought to stop.

In Aline B. Saarinen's delightful book about art collectors, "The Proud Possessors," she quotes Nelson Rockefeller talking about his father, John D. Rockefeller, Jr: "One of Father's favorite expressions . . . is 'The last five per cent is what counts.' His whole feeling is that if the last five per cent—the finish and the detail—are taken care of, everything else will come out all right." Rockefeller was thinking about the problems of a connoisseur judging works of art like Gothic tapestries and Chinese porcelains, but I think the phrase's applicability is wide. My subjects are inspired to finish what they are doing. It cannot be said that they go too far, but they are recklessly unconcerned about stopping when common sense would suggest that enough is enough. According to a recent issue of *Time* magazine, Paul Taylor, the director of the Paul Taylor Dance Company, made up the word "zunch" to express this idea in a memo to his troupe. "Zunch," he wrote, "is the magic that stays with the watchers after we are done. Zunch is opening up. Turning the burner on. Going beyond. Isn't that what makes a dancer out of a pedestrian?"

The language needed that word. Now that I have it, I can explain that "The Finishing Touch" is about the zunch of the last five per cent.

# CHAPTER 2

# Children's Best Seller

## MARGARET WISE BROWN

BETWEEN now and December 24 hundreds of thousands of mothers, grandmothers, uncles, brothers, and friends of young children will approach salesclerks in bookshops, toy stores, drug and department stores with minor variations of the stereotyped inquiry, "Which book would be best for my nephew, Theodore? He is 4 years old, but very advanced for his age." (No one has ever asked for a book for a backward nephew. Most publishers, therefore, lie in age-level advertisement; a book that should be a pushover for a Three is called suitable for a Four.) The chances are good that a customer, especially if he or she is looking for something in the $1 to $2.50 class,* will come away with one of Margaret Wise Brown's books.

---

*Inflation makes a mockery of these 1947 prices. In 1978 the prevailing prices for clothbound picture books, printed in color, are $4.95, $5.95, $6.95, and higher.

In the brief ten years Miss Brown has been writing for children she has had fifty-three books published, of which forty-seven are still in print and on sale under the imprints of seven different publishers. Miss Brown's total sales are, in round numbers, 836,000. A publishing house is usually reluctant to let any writer in its stable appear under another firm's colors. In Margaret Wise Brown's case, however, her seven publishers combined are unable to keep up with her output. To avoid flooding the market, Miss Brown has adopted three noms-de-plume. For Doubleday she is Golden MacDonald, author of the best sellers, *Little Lost Lamb, Red Light Green Light,* and *Big Dog Little Dog.* As Timothy Hay she is the author of Harper's *Horses.* Juniper Sage, printed by William R. Scott, is really Miss Brown and a collaborator, Edith Thacher Hurd. Harper and Scott also publish Miss Brown under her real name, but Doubleday believes that Golden MacDonald, who has written three smash hits in a row, now has greater sales appeal than Margaret Wise Brown and would be reluctant to drop the deception. Miss Brown manages to feel entirely free from jealousy toward her pseudonymous selves. She does think, however, that the Misses MacDonald, Hay, and Sage have clear-cut writing personalities and distinct styles, and has said that by the first draft of a new book it is perfectly clear in her mind who wrote it.

During the first two weeks of October, three new Brown books, all destined to be hits, appeared on the market. Doubleday published *The Little Island* by Golden MacDonald which, as a Junior Literary Guild selection, started off with a sale of 20,000. *The Man in the Manhole* by Juniper Sage (Miss Brown and Edith Thacher Hurd) is a most promising title on the new

Scott list. *Little Fur Family* by Margaret Wise Brown
(Harper), a miniature volume bound in New Zealand
rabbit fur, looked and felt so good that the publishers
ordered a huge first printing of 75,000 copies. Harper
is already planning a second edition in normal size and
texture and has published a limited (two copies,
valued at $15 each) mink edition for the carriage
trade.

In addition to her solid claim to the title of World's
Most Prolific Picture-Book Writer, Miss Brown, who is
unmarried, is probably prettier than any of her com-
petitors. She is a tall, green-eyed, ash blonde in her
early thirties with a fresh outdoors look about her.
People who meet her for the first time are likely to
think she is extremely sophisticated, which is entirely
true. Her striking appearance is usually punctuated by
some startling accessory such as a live kitten in a
wicker basket or a hat made out of live flowers, and is
emphasized nearly always by a high-spirited Kerry
blue terrier on a kelly green leash. Nominally she lives
in New York City. Actually she is away in Maine (where
she spends her summers), Connecticut, Long Island,
Vermont, or Virginia about half the time. She almost
never reads newspapers, depending for her information about current events upon whatever her friends
happen to tell her; nearly all subjects of major importance come up sooner or later, although occasionally
the time lag is fairly long. She did not hear about this
summer's stock-market crash, for example, until three
weeks afterward and for a while, on account of a fisher-
man's garbled report, Miss Brown understood that the
U.S. and Yugoslavia were at war.

Miss Brown, therefore, is likely to say things that in
simplicity and form have the surface glitter of an epi-

gram. A friend once asked her what time it was and Miss Brown replied, thoughtfully, "What time would you like it to be?" If you ask Miss Brown what her hobby is she will answer, probably, "Privacy." Many a stranger, afraid to ask her what the hell she was talking about, has taken such a remark home for study under the impression that Miss Brown combines the best features of Dorothy Parker and Immanuel Kant.

The first things Miss Brown can remember about her childhood are high grille fences and a red-brick church in Greenpoint, Brooklyn, where she was born. Her father, Robert Bruce Brown, was one of the heads of the prosperous American Manufacturing Company, makers of hemp rope, cordage, twine, and bagging. Margaret's mother came from a first Virginia family with a genealogy filled with Revolutionary War heroes.

The woods and beaches around Whitestone Landing, N. Y., where the Browns soon moved, were Margaret's favorite playground. She had thirty rabbits, ten squirrels, a bowl of goldfish, a collie of her own and six other "borrowed" dogs, but only three children to play with, not counting her brother who was really too old and her sister who was really too young.

In school and college Miss Brown was interested in those writers who, in the 1920s and early 1930, were experimenting with forms and techniques. She took a short-story course at Columbia but couldn't think up any plots. Then she decided to study at the Bureau of Educational Experiments in New York City, now known as Bank Street Schools.* It turned out to be the first step toward her picture-book writing career.

*It is now called the Bank Street College of Education.

Writing for young children looks easy. An entire book may contain three hundred words of text, or even less. The words are simple. It is not as easy as it looks, however, because children are a merciless audience. An author of picture books may fool publishers and adults some of the time; the unavoidable test is what happens when the child hears the story. Most of Miss Brown's fifty-three books, put to this trial, are a rollicking success. Her "noisy books" *(The City Noisy Book, The Country Noisy Book, The Seashore Noisy Book* and *The Indoor Noisy Book)* are written in sounds and questions that bring the child into the story. They concern a small blindfolded dog, Muffin, who trots around hearing noises: an automobile's "awuurraawuurra," an airplane's "rrrrr," a frog's "Jugar jugarum," a vacuum cleaner's "mmmzzmmmmmmmmmmm," or the hush of a very quiet custard. Nothing could be more fascinating to a four-year-old than listening to his parents' struggles with the vocal demands of the text or more hilarious than the books' surprise questions: "It began to snow. But could Muffin hear that?"

At the Bureau of Educational Experiments Miss Brown learned what will tickle small children, entertain, enchant, and make them jump. The Bureau, a hotbed of progressive-education theory directed by Lucy Sprague Mitchell, combines a model nursery school and student teachers' course. Miss Brown enrolled in the course and was soon offered a job on the publications staff. Her special duty was testing child reaction to writing for children, including some things of her own that Mrs. Mitchell had encouraged her to write.

It was not hard, when listening to one of her own stories read aloud, to tell when something adult or overwritten had crept in. In their own storytelling, moreover, "the little guinea pigs" suggested hundreds of ideas of things that they liked to hear about, favorite phrases, and intriguing patterns of words. A certain Mollie, for example, aged two, dictated this classic poem* to a Bank Street staff member:

> Remember the goldfish?
>   Remember?
> Remember the Goldfish?
>
> Goes round and round!
>   Umn!
> Swims?
>   Umn!
> Sleeps!
>   Umn!
>
> Remember the goldfish?
>   Has no hands.
>   No.
>   Has no feet.
>   No.
>
> Remember the goldfish?
>   Has no hands!
> Remember the goldfish?
>   Has no hands.

If it hadn't been for Bank Street and Mrs. Mitchell, Miss Brown might never have drifted into writing for children, yet the first book she wrote on her own represented a protest against Bank Street doctrine. Mrs. Mitchell believed fervently that a child's first five

*From *Another Here and Now Story Book*, edited by Lucy Sprague Mitchell. Published by E. P. Dutton & Co.

or six years of literary experience should be entirely in accord with his or her personal experiences; that children should be read stories about the familiar sights, smells, and sounds, postponing the traditional myths and classics, fairy tales and fables, for later on.

That premise pinched a little on Miss Brown's carefree imagination. Out of a Chekhov plot she made a story about an old, old lady with seventeen cats and one little blue-gray kitten who lived alone by the side of the sea and who, when the cold wind blew, was comforted by her kitten. Miss Brown tossed off the text, put it in the bottom of her desk and went off to Virginia for a week's vacation. While she was away one of her colleagues found the manuscript and took it to Harper & Brothers. They published it in 1937 without changing a word under the title, *When the Wind Blew*.

That was the first of Miss Brown's fifty-three books. Harper immediately published another of her stories, and at the same time Mr. Macrae of Dutton asked her to come and see him. "I had never seen a publisher before," Miss Brown says. "I was never more impressed." Mr. Macrae asked her to do a book for him. "How big a book?" Miss Brown asked. Mr. Macrae looked puzzled. "I mean," she explained, "how thick would it have to be?" Mr. Macrae said he thought a book of just ordinary thickness would do, and he sent an assistant for a sample.

Miss Brown looked at it thoughtfully and decided it was all right for size. She was on the point of accepting the commission when Mr. Macrae brought up the subject of money by offering an advance and a 12 1/2% royalty on retail sales. She didn't have the slightest idea what the figure meant, but instinctively asked for 15. That negotiation ended in the best contract Miss

Brown has ever signed. In later deals, despite far greater bargaining power, she has always settled for less.

In 1938 a fledgling publisher, William R. Scott, went to his friend Mrs. Mitchell and asked her to be children's book editor for his firm. Mrs. Mitchell was too busy, but she suggested Miss Brown. "I went to lunch," Miss Brown says, "and stayed for four years." As a Scott editor Miss Brown quickened the pace of her output. Within a year four Brown books appeared. Miss Brown also worked on a remarkable volume, *Cottontails*, designed for children as young as eighteen months. It was a tactile book, meant to be handled rather than read; the apple tree had red-glass buttons for apples, the bunny had a tuft of cotton for a tail and there was a bell on the cat's collar that really tinkled. In case the child, tired of playing with the book, tried to eat this literary fare that was quite all right because *Cottontails* was printed on untreated cloth with non-toxic dyes.

The "feely book" (as *Cottontails* was called) illustrates one of Miss Brown's writing principles: that it is valuable to appeal to *all* the senses of a very young audience. Five-year old children, she maintains, reach a peak of sensory awareness and she therefore likes the challenge of writing for them. After five, she says, the average child's perception, especially in touch, taste, and smell, begins to dull. "Once in a great while," Miss Brown says, "a five-year-old retains his awareness when he grows up and then he becomes either a painter, a writer or a poet."

Miss Brown also knows from experience that many children are more appreciative of art than their sense-

blunted parents. Children do not feel obliged to inter-
pret or explain and destroy thereby a painting's emotional content. Once Miss Brown was testing a series
of abstract paintings by showing reproductions to a
class of four-year-olds. The teacher, coming in suddenly, gazed in astonishment at a big bold abstraction
and said, "My goodness, what's that?" To which one
small boy, with characteristic progressive-school manners, replied impatiently. "It's a picture, you dope!"

Miss Brown imagined that Gertrude Stein's prose
would please children, and Mr. Scott, acting on that
inspiration, asked Miss Stein for a manuscript. He got,
as a result, the charming *The World Is Round* published
by Stein command on rose-colored paper with blue
ink. The day the manuscript arrived the Scott editors,
Miss Brown, Mr. Scott, and John McCullough, met at
Miss Brown's Greenwich Village apartment to see
what Miss Stein had produced. Miss Brown had forgotten to pay her electric bill and just as they were
starting to read the lights went out, so she lit candles.
As they read on it got late, so Miss Brown suggested
that they eat something. The only thing in her kitchen
was a giant cake in the shape of a boat which she had
ordered for a sailing enthusiast friend.

Miss Brown set the cake down before her friends
and they had eaten well into the prow when her broth-
er-in-law, Basil, a sober history professor at Barnard
College, arrived to return a borrowed vacuum cleaner.
He opened the door and saw by the flickering light the
three figures huddled around the boat. Miss Brown
was reading aloud: "Once upon a time the world was
round and you could go on it around and around.
Everywhere there was somewhere and everywhere

there they were men women children dogs cows wild pigs little rabbits cats lizards and animals . . ." Basil dropped the vacuum cleaner and bolted out the door.

The first draft of a Brown book is usually written in wild, enthusiastic haste in almost unintelligible soft pencil on whatever scraps of paper are available; the backs of grocery bills, shopping lists, old envelopes. "I finish the rough draft in 20 minutes," Miss Brown says, "and then I spend two years polishing." She is currently polishing twenty-three books more or less simultaneously.

"A picture book," Miss Brown says, "must be dramatic, and much of the drama is in turning over the pages." One dramatic device, recurrent in the collected Brown works, is contrast. The biggest noise on the street, the fire engine, is immediately followed by the sound, if any, of the sun shining. The foghorn is followed by the flutter of little birds' wings, the whistle of the ocean liner by a sailboat sailing by. Miss Brown also thinks a book should include at least a couple of words too big and cumbersome for her youthful listeners, a theory that drives many child psychologists, teachers and librarians, professionally committed to safe and sane age-level word lists, into shocked outrage. Miss Brown loves to tuck in words like "sanctimonious" and "ruminating," phrases like "by the incredible velvet that grows on your nose, you are a rapscallion cat." "I once read a book in French to the Threes," says Miss Brown with a note of triumph in her voice. "They couldn't understand a word. They loved every syllable."

The success of a picture book depends heavily on its design and illustration. Often text is entirely subor-

dinated to pictures. Part of Miss Brown's job is working with her illustrators, making sure that their work
matches her idea and mood. An outsider, eavesdrop-
ping on such a conference, might hear something like
this: "I like the rabbit, he has real sleepyness," "Yes,
but I'm worried about the yarn; it loses personality
and softness." "The chicken is fine. So many chickens
have no feathers. But I'm afraid you've got buttons for
daisies." "Let's drop a verse because that will give you
a chance to move out into the color double-spread; we
want plenty of air for the horses."

This kind of doubletalk is essential, probably, to
Miss Brown's work. Perhaps her hobby of painting in
oils, which she pursues with enthusiasm and incompe-
tence, helps her understand the artists' problems. But
she can be tough in demanding that the illustrations
live up to her preconceptions and thinks relatively
little of insisting that an entire set be redone.

In recognition, possibly, of the fact that her standards are high, Miss Brown voluntarily splits her royalties with the illustrator, a larger share of the kitty
than most artists expect or writers will grant. Her only
financial records are laboriously awkward penciled
notes in the end pages of her desk-size checkbooks.
She draws royalties on nearly fifty books, but has no
idea when the checks are due and is surprised, whenever one arrives, as if somebody had given her an
unexpected present. Her income, which currently is
about $10,000 a year, would be considerably larger if
it were not for a series of spectacularly bad bargains
she has made, selling her rights for token amounts or
giving them away for nothing. She sold *Baby Animals*
outright for $150 because at the time she needed $150
to buy a gray wolfskin jacket.

Except for clothes, champagne, and flowers, Miss
Brown hasn't much interest in spending money. She
moved from Greenwich Village, and lives alone in a
miniature Eighteenth Century wooden farmhouse,
Cobble Court, hidden away behind the houses in the
East Seventies in New York City* and, in the summer,
in a ghostly, isolated old house at Wharf's Quarry,
Vinal Haven, Maine, which, because it is the only one
of a few granite cutters' houses left standing, she calls
The Only House.

It is hard to decide which place is more unlikely. No
one would expect to find Cobble Court in the midst of
Manhattan's bustle and brownstone. On the other
hand it takes a flexible imagination to conceive of anybody voluntarily living in The Only House from May
to October, considering that it might fall down any
moment, that it has no bathroom, electricity, gas, heat,
telephone, or road and can only be approached by
small boat or airplane. Cobble Court has a living room
furnished in fur and a polished brick floor. But The
Only House can match that with a second-story door
which, from the inside, opens without warning onto a
sheer drop of twenty feet into the sea.

Miss Brown also likes to grow trees indoors. For a
while she had a green bay tree in her Greenwich Village apartment that she decorated like a Christmas
tree with white gardenias or fruits in season, fooling
many an arboreal ignoramus into thinking it, successively, a cherry tree, an orange tree, a pear tree, etc.
Her favorite outdoor sport is beagling, an esoteric

*Cobble Court was threatened by demolition a year or two ago, when the
whole block of buildings in front of it was torn down to make way for new
construction. Fortunately, someone who liked it as much as Margaret did
moved it, intact, to the West Village, where it still stands.

form of hunting. It consists of running cross-country in pursuit of a pack of beagles who, in turn, are supposed to be hot on the trail of Oklahoma jack rabbits especially imported for the chase. A beagler's object is to run fast enough to be in at the kill when the hounds finally catch up with their prey and, assuming that the pack has not torn the rabbit to bits before anyone can interfere, a successful beagler is rewarded by getting a rabbit's foot suitable for mounting. Miss Brown has several such gruesome trophies as evidence of her stamina and fleetfootedness.

Whenever anybody points out that beagling is an odd hobby for a woman who lives by writing books about the hopes and aspirations of small furry creatures, Miss Brown is likely to counter with: "Well, I don't especially like children, either. At least not as a group. I won't let anybody get away with anything just because he is little."

# CHAPTER 3

# My Table-Tennis Racket

*DICK MILES*

THE year was 1946. Joe Louis was the world's heavyweight champion. Ted Williams was the American League's most valuable player. Jack Kramer was monarch of men's lawn tennis. I was nearing the end of my first year as a full-time free-lance magazine writer.

I'd won no titles or honors. But I did hope to go on doing what I was doing. I liked it. I'd sold eight articles, which seemed to me to be an amazingly large number. Yet it was becoming increasingly hard to ignore what looked like a definite threat to my hope: my living expenses had been considerably larger than my total receipts. The money I had saved in the Army was almost all gone. And since I was already working seven days a week, as fast as I could urge my fingers to go, I felt I needed some improvement more subtle than promising myself to work harder. Even the beaver's eagerness has some natural limits.

For instance, I felt it would help to get better prices for articles. My biggest, most remunerative sale had been a piece for *Life*. I called on Robert Coughlan, then *Life's* text editor, thinking that it would be nice to wangle a second assignment from him. A sports personality close-up—an article about somebody on the order of, say, Louis, Williams, or Kramer—was the kind of thing I had in mind.

Coughlan looked profoundly bored. "We've got an awful lot of sports articles already in the works," he said. "On the other hand, we might be able to use something offbeat. Something light, on the amusing side."

My hopes were raised, if by less than one full millimeter. We talked for a while, trying to think of minor and peculiar sports. One of us—I don't remember which—brought up Ping-Pong.

"Is there a national Ping-Pong champion?" Coughlan asked.

"I think there must be," I said.

"Why don't you check?" Coughlan said. "It's just possible that he—if there is such a he—might make a piece."

It was an excellent suggestion, although it has taken me ten years to appreciate the value of Coughlan's advice. He was inviting me to latch onto as good a subject—in a way—as any freelance writer could desire. I fear I may never find another in quite the same class.

His name is Richard Miles. I found him in the Public Library under "T" for "Table Tennis." (I discovered that the United States Table Tennis Association detests the name "Ping-Pong" with the intensity that minority groups loathe ethnic slurs.) The champion,

PHILIPPE HALSMAN

Margaret Wise Brown in 1948 with her Kerry Blue, Crispian. *Right:* Writing (or pretending to write) at Cobble Court, Margaret's little farmhouse which was then (1947) on the upper East Side of Manhattan.

Margaret and her sister, Roberta (left), with Margaret's Collie and a few smaller animals.

Dick Miles.

Dick Miles is about to exe-
cute a forehand chop.

according to the magazine *Table Tennis Topics,* was a twenty-year-old New Yorker who had won the national men's singles crown in 1945, had defended his title successfully in the spring of 1946, and was favored to win for the third time in 1947. I asked Miles to have lunch with me, and in an offbeat way he was great. Not many national champions at any sport are likely to joke about their game. Miles, a small, trim fellow with the indefinable air of titleholder about him, took a delightfully mocking view both of himself and table tennis. He said he thought that his game, for its size, was a lot of fun, but that for real challenge he recommended golf. While he enjoyed being champion, he said he preferred reading James Joyce or listening to Beethoven quartets.

When I turned in my article about Miles, *Life* seemed pleased with it. They promptly sent me a check for $1000 that made my bank account look markedly less forlorn. They scheduled the piece for an early issue and assigned Gjon Mili, one of the magazine's top photographers, to take multiple-exposure photographs of Miles in action. Everyone involved seemed happy, including the United States Table Tennis Association, which felt that the game was about to get an unusual but richly deserved publicity break.

A day or two before the article should have gone to press, Miles and I were summoned to inspect the photographs. The champion's strokes, which were very fast indeed, had been too fast even for Mili's stroboscopic lights. The pictures were fascinating as abstract compositions of light patterns against a dark background. But there was simply no telling what they showed.

"They look like X-ray plates to me," Miles said, "and I'm afraid I may have broken my collarbone."

It was too late to take another batch of photographs in time to make the issue. The Miles story had to be held out. Coughlan thought it might be rescheduled after the forthcoming tournament—provided, of course, that Miles managed to keep his title.

Miles hid his disappointment well. "I'll do my best to win—just for the article's sake, of course," he said.

Miles's best was exceedingly good. He won the title for the third time, a feat only one other player, Lou Pagliaro, had ever managed. But *Life,* by late March, had cooled toward table tennis. Coughlan was very gentle in explaining to me that the editors had decided to forget about my piece.

"You can have it back. You can keep the money, but the article is yours. We realize that the manuscript is highly perishable, but there's certainly a chance that you can place it somewhere else."

That seemed more than fair—although I did hate to tell Miles, who would have to inform the Table Tennis Association, that our joint hopes had taken a severe jolt.

I took the article to Tim Cohane, sports editor of *Look,* and told him what had happened at *Life.* He didn't believe me. I got a written statement from Coughlan saying that the manuscript was all mine, free and clear, and that *Life* had no intention of printing anything about Dick Miles in the foreseeable future. Cohane still looked suspicious, feeling, I think, that some obscure inter-picture-magazine joke was being played on him. But to my delight he bought the article. Its text was just the same as originally, but I had updated it, of course, to include Miles's third victory. I got a check for $500.

"We want some good pictures to run with it," Cohane told me. "Frank Bauman, one of our top photographers, is going to take them."

I felt good. The extra check, for just a few hours spent on revision, was wholly welcome. But my pleasure was more than purely commercial. By this time, Miles and I were friends. I'd watched him practicing, worrying, winning for a year. I'd hung around with table-tennis buffs long enough to agree with them that the reading public hardly ever appreciates how very good a national champion has got to be. I was anxious to see the piece in print for Dick's sake as well as my own.

Bauman's photographs turned out beautifully—especially a posed shot of Miles, shot upwards from around his ankles, with his teeth bared, in which the mild-mannered champion looked positively tigerish. The picture was so dramatic, in fact, that *Look* turned the whole project into a one-page, one-picture feature, which it ran shortly before the 1948 championships. My deathless 3800 words of prose had been boiled down to a succinct 200-word caption. My byline had been omitted.

While I was trying to console myself with the thought that at least the spread was good publicity for Dick, he was battling his way to his fourth successive victory. That set an all-time table-tennis record. I reread the carbon of my article. And for the first time the low, sneaky thought crossed my mind that perhaps there was an advantage to having magazines *not* print the Miles story. For there was the champion, his luster brighter than ever. And there was I with a ready-made manuscript—slightly dog-eared, but virtually intact—telling all about him.

By this time my fortunes as a free-lancer had improved. I was breaking even. Still I listened with greedy fascination whenever more successful magazine writers explained their professional strategies. It sometimes seemed as if there were as many "how to" theories as there were surviving free-lancers. I had heard that the secret was to specialize doggedly in one narrow field in order to get a maximum wordage out of a minimum of research and reporting. I'd been advised to get out of town ("Any New York editor will buy anything if the dateline is Lawton, Oklahoma!") and to stick as close as possible to the New York Public Library ("After all, every magazine article is just a rewrite of stuff in the back-issue files!"). One well-fed writer told me that numbers were the trick of the game; if you couldn't work a number into the title ("Seven Sure Ways to Success"), then, at the very least, you should make a minimum of three numbered points, in boldface, in the body of the piece, and that three, ten, and one hundred, in his experience, were the best numbers to use. Another craftsman assured me that, when in doubt, a free-lancer should always do a test-yourself quiz ("Are You a Considerate Spouse?"); for it, he said, is the basic staple of magazine journalism.

I'd heard countless other systems explained, yet no one had mentioned my particular racket: the imperishable manuscript. For all I knew, I had stumbled onto an original tactic. I began to think, giddily, that if I could sell the Miles story once or twice every year . . .

At any rate there could be no harm, all pipe dreams

aside, in trying one more time. All my article needed, as far as I could see, was minor updating.

*Esquire's* articles editor, when I suggested the idea of a piece on Dick Miles to him, looked intrigued. He had been looking for an offbeat sports personality story. What had happened at *Life* and *Look,* I gathered, amused him. I added the latest Miles news to the old text structure, retyped, kept my fingers crossed, and in late June, 1948, *Esquire* bought the article for $400.

In February, 1949—to my astonishment—*Esquire* printed almost the whole thing, with photographs, under the title "Young Man on the Ball."

All of us were pleased: Miles, the Table Tennis Association, and I. For even though my desk drawer did look strangely empty, and though it was with a certain twinge that I crossed the note to myself, "Miles piece, where?" off my memo pad, I felt I ought to be realistic about the matter. No champion, after all, can win forever. Now that Dick was twenty-four, he had taken to calling himself "The Grand Old Man" of table tennis and to predicting his imminent dethronement. "I'm beginning to like playing as much as winning," Miles said. "And of course, in a champion, that's fatal." Prudence suggested that I close my books on Miles as an article subject. Three sales on what was, in substance, one article were clearly as good mileage as a writer could want from a manuscript.

Miles defaulted in 1950, after winning in 1949. He made a comeback in 1951. But in 1952, for the first time in eight years, he was beaten in the nationals. It was just for old times' sake, he said, that he entered the 1953 tournament. When he won his seventh championship that year, I wondered. In 1954 he raised the total to eight. Counting back on the calendar, I realized that it had been five years since a piece (mine) about him had been printed in any of the general magazines.

Then Dick appeared as a guest on the television show "I've Got a Secret." His secret was that he was the national table-tennis champion. The panel was almost stumped. Even after it had learned that Miles was a champion at something that had to do with a table, the experts were making wild guesses. "Champion pie-eater?" somebody asked. I saw that Miles, despite my best efforts, was less celebrated than he deserved.

*Sports Illustrated* was getting ready to start publication. I dropped in to see Andrew Crichton, one of its editors.

"We're interested, among other things, in offbeat sports personality pieces," Crichton explained. I couldn't resist. Crichton thought it sounded like a funny idea.

I hurried home, dug out all my old carbons and notes, and tackled the Miles story for the fourth time. It was a completely new manuscript. For one thing, a new racquet surface (sponge instead of pebbled rubber) had been invented since the last go-around, so I had to bring the article abreast of the game's technological changes. Yet the piece did bear some unavoidable similarities to the three earlier versions. There was nothing I could do, after all, to vary the facts about Dick's birthplace, schooling, and early sports career.

Crichton liked it. I got a prompt letter of acceptance and a check for $750. I wrote back and said that while the article ought to stand up for a good six months, I did hope *Sports Illustrated* would run it before the 1955 tournament, since I naturally couldn't promise that

the eight-time winner, good as he was, would pull off
a ninth victory.

Crichton advised me not to worry. The piece wasn't
exactly scheduled, he said, but it was well liked.

A couple of months later I got a call from a *Sports
Illustrated* researcher, a girl with a mellifluous voice.
"We were wondering," she cooed, "whether anybody
has taken any good photographs of Miles."

I felt it was a bad omen. I was hardly surprised, when
the weekend of the 1955 nationals had passed, that
*Sports Illustrated* confined its coverage to the results,
printed in its smallest type size. The winner (for the
ninth time): Richard Miles.

Not long afterwards, I saw Dick. "I sure am sorry
about the *Sports Illustrated* business," I said.

"Don't worry about it," Dick said.

"That's magazines for you," I said.

"It really makes no difference to me," Dick said.
"Although I imagine that the Table Tennis Association is sort of disappointed."

"Of course," I said, "there's a chance that something can be salvaged. You are still the champion,
after all. Now if I were just to bring the article up
to date . . ."

Dick looked at me reproachfully. "I hate to tell
you," he said, "but I've decided to let the title go."

I hated to hear it.

Miles didn't enter the 1956 championships, which
were held in March at White Plains, New York. The
men's singles title went to the junior champion, Irwin
"Ginger" Klein. It's conceivable—hard as it is for me
to face—that Dick has really and truly retired.

And yet I wonder. A man who has won a championship nine times must be tempted—if only for tidiness'

sake—to try to make it a round number like ten.

I'll admit I'd like to see Dick try. I wouldn't be surprised if he could do it. A man who has sold an article four times naturally wonders whether he couldn't make it five.

\*

In 1962, Miles came out of his retirement, entered the men's singles, and won the championship for the tenth time, an extraordinary record. I cannot say that I failed to sell my article a fifth time, because I did not try to. For one thing, *Sports Illustrated* had not returned my manuscript. And then, when I looked back on the 1949 *Esquire* version, I realized that it had contained most of what I had to say about table tennis as Dick Miles played it. For the sake of the record, this is the *Esquire* version:

There are millions of table-tennis tables in the United States, and each of them comes equipped with its own champion—the guy, or sometimes the girl, who regularly whips all comers. Taken as a group, table-tennis enthusiasts are a happy and agile (if slightly breathless) band. Their cheeks are pink. Their eyes sparkle with the excitement of victory. They are confident and alert.

It's just as well, though, that most of them have no idea what really good table tennis is like; and it's fortunate, in particular, that almost none of them has ever played against a young man named Dick Miles. Miles is the United States men's singles table-tennis champion and, without serious doubt, the best player that this country has ever developed. He has a way of discouraging those who do battle against him.

The gap between championship table tennis and the

common, or basement gameroom, variety is just as wide as the difference between lawn tennis as Riggs and Kramer play it and an ordinary Sunday afternoon of sociable mixed doubles. But while the average tennis player knows quite well how far his skill falls short of championship calibre, the average table-tennis player lives in contented ignorance. "Most of them don't even know how the game is supposed to look," Miles explains. "It's pretty funny that with so many Americans playing table tennis, they're all so unsophisticated about the game."

Quite a number of the lawn-tennis stars fancy themselves good table-tennis players, perhaps because they think of it as a funny midget version of their big specialty. Recently, one of them who is famous for his cockiness on and off the court dropped in at the Broadway Table Tennis Courts, where Miles generally plays and practices. The tennis champ thought his table tennis was pretty hot. He wanted to play Miles. He was willing to make a small wager that he could beat Miles.

"You wouldn't have a chance," said Miles. "I could even beat you sitting down."

The tennis star, insulted, doubled his bet. Somebody produced a high stool of the kitchen type and Miles perched on it, two or three feet back from his end of the table. The lawn-tennis man was not bad; he simply had no conception of the intricate technique involved in top-flight table tennis. He played as if it were merely lawn tennis that had been left in vinegar overnight and had shrunk in size. Miles took him handily in three straight games.

Championship table tennis doesn't look awfully tough to a spectator. You notice Miles and his colleagues don't pay much attention to their serves. The fraternity-house champion is likely to have a power-house serve, a low sizzler with a nasty twist of some kind; the U.S. men's singles champion, on the other hand, merely puts the ball in play with a low-bouncing but unaggressive shot. This is because, since 1933, the rules have outlawed such devilish inventions as the finger-spin serve, which in experts' hands had become almost unreturnable; the chances are that the fraternity-house champion, without knowing it, violates the rules of the game. The ball must be held on the flat palm, fingers outstretched, thumb free; tossed into the air, and struck onto the server's side of the net, over the net, and onto the receiver's court. These restrictions keep top-flight players from cutting or hitting hard enough to force their opponents into error; and so, by convention, the serve has practically vanished as an offensive weapon.

You notice, secondly, that while the table-tennis experts play farther back from the table than you probably do, they're not as far back as posed publicity pictures would have you believe. They *can* go way back, it's true. On occasion, Miles will bound backward as much as forty feet and still manage to make the return. He would greatly prefer not to do so, however, because it means he has been forced back. A table-tennis ball, which weighs less than one-eighth of an ounce, slows down suddenly when the force of a drive is spent. An agile expert, therefore, can beat a hasty retreat and get shots which, as they careened off the table, were going too fast to see, much less return. But it's a last, desperate resort.

What you can't observe—and the part of championship table tennis that the lawn-tennis star is likely to underestimate—is the importance of spins, cuts, and chop shots. You have to play Miles to understand their full significance.

You face the champion across nine feet of green table. He looks quite friendly. He explains his repertory of strokes, showing you, for example, a thing he calls the forehand chop, which looks a lot like the action involved in hammering a nail. Then: "All right," he says. "Now when I chop the ball at you, it has a tendency to come off your racquet into the net. Let's try a few."

It sounds fine, and you entertain the secret idea that perhaps you'll be able to pull off one of your super-smashes and make a monkey out of the champ. Miles floats the ball over the net right to your forehand. You knock it back to Miles. You notice, vaguely, that on the third shot Miles has employed that hammer-and-nail business, but the ball comes toward you nice and easy and tempting. You swing gracefully.

Now you begin to see what Miles has been talking about. You hit the ball all right, but it dribbles off your racquet and poofs into the net. On the next try you aim higher; the ball goes right for the net. You play ten points and, feeling like a fool, you net every one of Miles' chop shots.

"It's the backspin," Miles says soothingly. "You want to watch it." But you can't even see it. Then Miles proceeds to show you how he can make you hit out or off to the left or off to the right. He tells you in advance which blunder you are going to commit. Like a dumb sheep, you make the mistake just as predicted.

"Of course, if I mix them up without telling you," Miles says, "it starts to get kind of complicated." He hits one to you. It looks like a chop, and you aim for the ceiling to make sure you'll clear the net. It wasn't a chop. You hit the ceiling.

"I see what you mean," you say, and resolve to keep the whole thing strictly on a conversational plane from now on.

Whatever loss of self-esteem you may have suffered, you have gained some insight into the skill that has enabled Dick Miles, at twenty-two, to overshadow the U.S. table-tennis scene. Miles is the first four-time winner of the national title in the game's history. He has won four times in a row and will undoubtedly be a favorite to make it five this year. He is a three-time winner of the Eastern Championships. He has won the New York City title four successive times. He is, with Miss Thelma Thall of Columbus, Ohio, the present world's mixed-doubles champion. For the past two years he has been number-one man on the U.S. Swaythling Cup Squad, table tennis' equivalent of the Davis Cup team, and he is also number one on the New York City team, perennial winner of the national intercity championships. Readers of the magazine *Table Tennis Topics,* official publication of the United States Table Tennis Association, recently voted by a wide margin that Miles was the "greatest player the United States has ever produced."

Miles doesn't look much like an all-time champion. He is small (5'7"), light (122 lbs.), and rather pale. He has curly black hair, dark brown eyes, and an ingratiating, wistful smile. His hands are small and sensitive. His right forearm is conspicuously muscular; otherwise his sports career, as far as one can see, has done nothing for his physique. Nevertheless, there is a self-conscious assurance about the way he moves. It is clear that Miles, despite his quiet and his reserve, re-

gards the world with something of the disdain he
holds for a high-bouncing return by a clumsy opponent.

Miles affects an easygoing mien, but in reality he is
about as composed as a race horse waiting in the starting gate. He stands at the table with a slight slouch,
relaxed and looking somewhat abstracted, but his high
nervous-energy potential is revealed in the hair-trig-
ger speed of his reactions and, at tight moments, by a
quick gesture of impatience. He holds his hands parallel in front of his chest and shakes them ever so
slightly, as if to say, *sotto voce,* "For God's sake, Miles,
let's not slop around."

The champion loves table tennis and loves to win.
At the same time, though, he thinks there is a definite
limit to legitimate enthusiasm over any sport. He is
aware that the world is full of a number of other
things; and two of the other things that interest him
most, just now, are Beethoven chamber music and
James Joyce. He says he'd rather play the piano than
table tennis, and has arranged to swap lessons with a
young concert pianist, Bernard Baslow, who feels exactly the other way around. Miles' room in his family's
apartment on New York's Riverside Drive is crowded
in about equal measure with table-tennis trophies and
albums of classical records. Several years ago, a sports
writer on the New York *Post* told Miles that he ought
to read Joyce's *A Portrait of the Artist as a Young Man,*
and Miles followed the advice. "I have never been the
same since," he says. He is now in the middle of *Finne-
gans Wake.* As far as Miles knows, he is the first table-
tennis champion with any interest at all in Irish literature.

The champion first began to play in 1938. He was

thirteen, a high-school freshman. He started playing simply because there was a table-tennis emporium at 79th Street and Broadway, right on his way home from school.

Once he tried it, he liked it, and after a couple of years, he was good enough to beat most of the 79th Street set. Then somebody persuaded him to try his luck at the curious establishment known as "1721 Broadway," which is the focal point for table tennis in the metropolitan area. By a process of mutual self-help, the 1721 Broadway regulars have long enjoyed the same kind of quasi monopoly in table tennis that Southern California has in lawn tennis. At the moment, for example, the five leading players in the country are all 1721 Broadway boys, which makes it pretty hard to get up a really first-class match in any other city. Twice a week, Tuesday and Friday nights, there are tournaments—a handicap affair Tuesday and a straight elimination contest Friday—which anybody can enter for a fee of one dollar. Miles began to play in these events and for a year or so he got trounced on a twice-a-week schedule, but by the best players in the U.S. Lou Pagliaro was then champion, and "Paggy" helped Miles more than anybody else. "Paggy" needed a practice partner, and fifteen-year-old Miles was overwhelmed with delight at being allowed to knock himself out as Pagliaro's foil.

In October, 1941, Miles entered the Brooklyn Championships, his first major competition. Before anybody quite realized what was happening, Miles had beaten Sol Schiff and Tibor Hazi, who ranked sixth and fourth nationally, and had pushed national doubles champion Ed Pinner to extra games in the semifinals. The table-tennis world buzzed with excitement.

The New York *Sun* said Miles was "the gold nugget" of the tournament. Everybody was astonished except Pagliaro, who knew his protégé had developed fast—and Miles, who couldn't see how he had let Pinner beat him.

Then in 1945 Miles got really hot. He won most of the important tournaments that come ahead of the Nationals, which are held annually in a different city around April 1st. He was favored to take the U.S. championship, and he justified the pretournament odds by winning in a breeze. There were those, however, who belittled Miles' victory in 1945 on the ground that many of the country's best players had been in the armed forces and had not yet had time to bring their drives and chops up to prewar standard. Miles had been kept out of the Army because of a heart murmur.

One reason for such anti-Miles propaganda was the champion's habit of making his victories look deceptively easy. Previous titleholders had been far more colorful—Schiff with his all-out concentration on the offense; Pagliaro, "The Terrible Midget," who raced around like a demon possessed and could return anything anybody hit at him. Miles, by contrast, seemed to take it easy, favoring neither the defense nor the offense, and often winning without apparent effort. From the gallery's viewpoint, the closest thing to a Miles specialty was his forehand drive in which he whipped his racquet around in a complete circle and banged the ball away with dazzling speed—a shot Miles liked to use to finish off a game, a signature to remind opponents that struggle was hopeless. Actually, Miles' secret weapon was a well-rounded game combined with unbelievably sharp anticipation. He had no real weakness for an opponent to attack. He gave the impression of casualness because he was a split second ahead of his rivals. He seldom had to scramble after a shot because, more often than not, he was in position waiting for it.

The 1946 championships showed the skeptics. The field of 149 players included every past U.S. titleholder. All had had plenty of time to get ready. Miles waltzed through the tournament almost effortlessly. He lost only one game en route, and he smothered Schiff in the finals 21–10, 21–10, 21–10. Quite a few of those who had questioned the champ's ability now began to grumble that Miles was *too* good and that he was hurting organized table tennis by taking all the element of doubt out of tournament play. Miles won for the third time in 1947, tying the record that Pagliaro had set in 1940, 1941, and 1942.

It was probably lucky for Miles that he went abroad in 1947 to represent the United States in the world championships in Paris and got himself soundly beaten. It proved that he was human, thus scotching in advance any suggestion that Miles ought to be made to play left-handed or blindfolded in order to restore an element of competition to the game. In preparation for the international play Miles picked a gangling seventeen-year-old, Martin Reisman, as a practice partner. Miles has done for Reisman what Pagliaro did for Miles, and while Miles finds a certain amount of ironic pleasure in the parallel, he wishes that his protégé had not learned his lessons quite so well: Reisman in the past two years has become Miles' most serious rival in the United States and the chief threat to the security of the champion's crown.

So far, both Reisman and Miles have failed to bring

home either the Swaythling Cup for team play or the singles championship. But Miles and Thelma Thall won the mixed doubles championship last year—the second time the United States has ever captured a world title. The USTTA has high hopes for this year, when, barring some startling upset, Miles and Reisman will represent the United States again; it is not impossible, given a lucky draw, that there will be an all-American finals.

One threat to the realization of that rosy dream is the danger that Miles and Reisman, in the meantime, will wear each other down to a frazzle. As soon as they got home from London in 1948, they played in the U.S. nationals and, true to form, met in the finals. It was, perhaps, the best match in U.S. table-tennis history. Miles and Reisman stood even at two games apiece. In the fifth and deciding game they tied at 20–20. The points seemed interminable. One lasted eight minutes, long enough for many an entire game. Miles finally beat his former pupil, thus retaining his title and setting a new all-time record of four successive victories. But when it was done, Miles was too exhausted to speak. Reisman could have been scraped off the floor with a table-tennis paddle.

Miles wonders how long he will be able to keep Reisman under control. He speculates eagerly about becoming the first American to win the world championship. But there is a third question that intrigues him too: is it possible to earn a living at the game?

The words "professional" and "amateur" are not mentioned in table-tennis circles. There are no such things. There are only "registered" players—players of some repute and skill who are in good standing with the USTTA—and so there is no table-tennis equivalent for the larger game's opprobrious "tennis bum."

Table-tennis experts are entirely free to make as much money as they choose out of the game: the trick is in figuring out a way to do so. The only man who has solved the puzzle with real success is Coleman Clark, an exhibition player, who appears regularly in theatres, night clubs, and at sports shows. Clark has found it hard work. Miles is both impressed and depressed by the fact that Clark, in a ten-year period, has worn out an estimated total of 24,500 table-tennis balls.

Despite all discouragement, Miles hopes soon to make a tidy sum out of a coast-to-coast tour, under USTTA auspices, with England's Richard Bergman, the current world champ, as his opponent. Their matches will be real contests, free from trick stuff—a miniature version, in fact, of the recent Riggs-Kramer rivalry. Miles has very little intention of letting Bergman run away with the series.

"Naturally I figure as the underdog," says Miles. "After all, Bergman is the titleholder. On the other hand, I have beaten him once or twice. It is just possible that I will be able to teach him a thing or two. I mean, of course, about James Joyce!"

\*

During all the years Miles dominated the game, the U.S. Table Tennis Association lamented the fact that so few Americans took the sport sufficiently seriously. One of Miles's most exciting table-tennis adventures occurred long after his reign as champion, when he had taken to writing about table tennis and other sports, mostly for *Sports Illustrated.* As a writer he was careful, as always, not to call table tennis by anything less than its official name. In April, 1971, the People's Republic of China, taking advantage of the fact that the U.S. had relaxed its travel restrictions, invited an American team to visit. Miles went along as a combination coach-correspondent, and thus played a part in the creation of the phrase— which must gall the Table Tennis Association, though not necessarily for foreign-policy reasons— "Ping-Pong Diplomacy."

# $\mathscr{P}$iano $\mathscr{M}$an

## *WILLIAM HUPFER*

$\mathscr{T}$HE nearest William Hupfer ever came to being a professional musician was in the summer of 1913, when, as a high-school student, he played the piano with a dance orchestra in a resort hotel at Lake George. Nowadays, although he occasionally sits down at the baby grand in the living room of his home —the lower half of a two-family frame house in the East Bronx—and raps out one of the Chopin études, he is woefully out of practice, as he has been for years. Unpromising though this background may seem, it is probably safe to say that, season in and season out, Hupfer contributes to the enjoyment of more concert and recital devotees, almost none of whom are even aware of his existence, than any other one individual in the musical world. As the head tone regulator for the piano-making firm of Steinway & Sons, Hupfer not only auditions and approves every concert grand that leaves the Steinway factory, in Long Island City, but

sees to it that the tone of each of the hundred and
thirty-one pianos the company keeps on hand in New
York to lend to musicians for concerts and recitals is
everything it should be. In the basement of Steinway
Hall, on West Fifty-seventh Street, where he is almost
constantly at work currying one or another of the
pianos in his lending stable, he receives about sixteen
hundred visits a year from musicians who, faced with
the ordeal of an appearance at Town Hall, Carnegie
Hall, or some other awesome auditorium, want the
comforting assurance that, whatever pitfalls may await
them, their piano is not going to be one of them.
Hupfer, although he officially takes the position that
any Steinway under his care is just as good as any
other, diplomatically succeeds in making practically
every one of them feel that he has picked the best of
the hundred and thirty-one—a feeling that has often
added lustre to a performance.

The importance of Hupfer's work stems from a
long-established Steinway business policy. A domi-
nant theme in the company's advertising is that many
prominent musicians admire its instruments, and it
frequently backs this up by quoting some artist on the
subject. (Vladimir Horowitz: "I am happy that the
Steinway has been my inseparable and faithful friend
in all countries since the very inception of my concert
career.") The company, which is old-fashioned in certain respects, does not believe in paying for such testimonials. It won't even help a musician draft one, with
the result that sometimes an intended compliment
sounds almost peevish. (Fritz Reiner: "Happy is he
who can afford a Steinway!") Obviously, if Hupfer
were to let his pianos deteriorate—or, as he says,
"start sounding like someone dropping an armful of

firewood"—the number of Steinway's happy friends
would dwindle and the source of its free endorse-
ments disappear. Such negligence would also wreck
the firm's considerable investment in its piano-lending
service and thereby scuttle another of its advertising
techniques. This service is unique in its scope, for in
addition to the hundred and thirty-one Steinway
grands available in New York, the company has almost
four hundred others spotted around the country in the
showrooms of strategically located Steinway dealers,
and stands ready to deliver a freshly dusted piano in
good voice to any concert hall or recital studio in the
United States for only the cost of moving it—an average, in Manhattan, of fifty-five dollars.* Anybody may
use this service, no matter how well or how dreadfully
he or she plays the piano, with one not very surprising
exception: The individual must not have endorsed the
product of some other piano manufacturer. In return
for its trouble and expense, Steinway expects its clients to insert a credit line—"Steinway," "Steinway
Piano," or, in the case of accompanists, "At the Steinway"—in their programs, and in all their handbills,
posters, and other advertisements as well. The credit-
line type is often small, but it's there—tens of thousands of times each season. Big as Steinway's service
has become, it has a continuing tendency to snowball,
for since no rival firm maintains a piano-lending library of comparable dimensions and since house
pianos in the hinterland are felt to be risky proposi-
tions, musicians who travel a lot are likely to find
themselves drawn almost willy-nilly into the family of

*Multiply by three and you will have the 1978 cost equivalent, or close to
it.

Steinway borrowers. In the end, this generally makes them happy, too, though it is not always easy to tell from their testimonials whether it is the tone of the piano or the efficiency of the service that has charmed them more. "Many happy things happen during a concert tour, but the apogee of delightful anticipation is reached when I know that I shall see a Steinway as I walk onto the various platforms," wrote the violist William Primrose, presumably for nothing.

Hupfer does not tune pianos. He sometimes says he does, but only to avoid complicated explanations arising from the fact that few people have ever heard of tone regulating—or "voicing," as it is often called in piano circles. He is a qualified tuner, all right, having tuned pianos for Steinway for thirty years before he was promoted to his present post, in 1946, and having travelled on the road for one fifteen-year stretch as personal tuner to one or another of several eminent pianists, Rachmaninoff, Hofmann, and Hess among them. For that matter, he is qualified in all phases of piano care, and has worked at every job a piano mechanic can hold. "I am what you might call an all-round piano man," Hupfer once said, with an emphasis that showed he thinks a lot more of versatility than of specialization. In emergencies, he still tunes a note here and there and oils a squeaky pedal, but for the most part he leaves all the chores of piano upkeep except regulating to assistants. Tone regulating is more difficult than tuning and entirely distinct from it. A regulator pays no attention to the strings, which are the tuner's chief concern, and concentrates on the condition of the hammer felts. His work demands extraordinarily acute hearing. A tuner listens for variations in pitch, which are relatively easy to spot; a regulator listens for variations in tone quality so subtle that both Paderewski and Rachmaninoff claimed they couldn't detect them. A tuner has a mechanical standard, a tuning fork, to keep him on the right track; a regulator is guided by nothing but memory. He must at some time in his life have been taught good tone by another regulator, and he must have kept the concept in his mind the way a housewife, for instance, keeps in mind the color of her walls at home while hunting a matching fabric in a department store. Hupfer, who learned correct tone from his predecessor, Joseph Messerschmitt, now sixty-six years old and retired, is Steinway's final authority on the subject; he embodies the ideal for the company, much as the international kilogram embodies a perfect unit of weight for the International Bureau of Weights and Measures. When Steinway & Sons wants to know how a piano sounds, it asks Hupfer. The firm turns out approximately two hundred and fifty concert grands a year, and Hupfer visits the plant once or twice a week to check on the tone of each new one before it is placed on the market. If a tonal problem comes up outside New York and the local Steinway experts can't solve it, Hupfer usually goes to the scene as a trouble-shooter, carrying a few small tools in a leather case but with most of his equipment in his head. On such trips, he may not have to do any repair work at all on the suspect piano; sometimes local feeling has turned capriciously against an instrument when in fact—meaning in Hupfer's opinion—nothing is wrong. When this happens, his reassuring word, perhaps accompanied by a few *pro-forma* gestures of adjustment, is usually enough to persuade everybody concerned that the piano sounds tiptop.

Hupfer does not claim that he has absolute pitch. He despises the phrase, partly because when proud mothers come into the basement to help their prodigies pick a piano, they always use it. "Pin down anybody who claims to have absolute pitch—to be able to tell precisely how many times a note vibrates in a second—and it usually turns out that at best they can identify a note as being, for instance, A," Hupfer once said. "But they haven't the faintest idea whether it's a 440, a 444, or a 448! What good is that?" Hupfer can tell an A when he hears one, but since he has to use a tuning fork to be positive of its exact pitch, he thinks this ability isn't worth mentioning. "However, I can usually tell the name of the piece and its composer," he says. "And for a piano man that's not bad."

A pianist who wants to borrow a Steinway for a New York performance makes an appointment with Hupfer through the latter's superior, Alexander Greiner, the head of Steinway's Concert and Artist Department, who, from his office on the third floor of Steinway Hall, where he keeps a large wall map of the United States studded with colored pins showing the disposition of the company's lending-library resources, makes sure that pianists all over the country get pianos when they want them and in the condition they want them. Greiner directs the applicant to Hupfer's basement workshop, a loftlike room seventy feet long and thirty feet wide. There are other rooms in the basement, among them two practice studios and a number that are used by Steinway's organ department, but Hupfer's workshop is nevertheless called the Basement, as if all the rest of the space could be ignored. The Basement is a plain, utilitarian place with a wide sliding door, a bare floor made of wooden blocks on which piano-leg casters roll easily, and a high ceiling cluttered with exposed steampipes and tin ventilator ducts. Its walls are painted in schoolroom style—dark green from the floor up to waist height and a dingy cream above. There are no windows, and the lighting is dim except in one corner, where a bright work light hangs down over a wooden carpenter's bench. The room's only decorative distinction is its contents—about twenty, usually, of the hundred and thirty-one lending pianos; the others, at any given time, are either out on loan or stored in auxiliary space on the second floor. All are either one or the other of the two largest models the company makes—the six-foot-eleven-inch Model B and the eight-foot-eleven-and-a quarter inch Model D—and all are a dignified black, with what the trade calls an "ebonized" surface, which, if scratched, can be easily touched up. They make an impressive display lined up there in the half-light—two elephantine rows of them, with their tops down and their keyboards facing in on what amounts to a center aisle.

The average borrower comes to the Basement in an apprehensive frame of mind, agitated by the prospect of having to face the New York critics within a couple of weeks and determined to pick out the very best piano in the place. Hupfer is sympathetic. Each piano in the Basement has an index number inscribed inside its case, and while an instrument is awaiting a borrower, a wooden frame containing a card on which this number has been crayoned is set on its top for easy identification; when the piano goes out on loan, its card is filed in a rack near the door. Hupfer has been known to claim that if the index numbers were erased and the cards were shuffled, no one would know which piano was which. Actually, the pianos differ enough so that Hupfer can tell them apart without their numbers, but he contends that by the time he and his staff have them properly adjusted, the differences between them are too minute for most people to detect, and he makes a point of acting as if all his pianos were interchangeable, even though he knows they aren't. Hupfer does not go into this subject in dealing with the average Basement client; he knows enough about the artistic temperament to realize it would be hopeless to try to persuade a jittery pianist that he could just as safely order his Steinway by telephone. "Confidence is the main thing," he says. "It doesn't matter which piano an artist picks—when Rubinstein plays them, they all sound great. But the artist should be completely confident that for him his choice is right. He should think to himself, Now, if there's one thing I don't have to worry about, it's the piano."

Both Hupfer's manner and his appearance make for confidence among his clients. He is a stocky man of fifty-six, with a square jaw, generous, dramatically black eyebrows, and—everything considered—highly ordinary-looking ears, and there is a trace of melancholy in his normal expression, somehow suggesting that he understands the tribulations of the concert business and the trials of the concert performer. At the same time, he looks dependable and has about him the assured air of one who has thoroughly resolved the mysteries of his craft. He says "How do you do?" to novices and "Hello!" to old customers with a combination of warmth and modest hesitancy, as if meeting a piano player, any piano player, were an enjoyable treat. He wears a white carpenter's apron over a white

shirt and the trousers of a business suit, and throughout the negotiations he sticks doggedly to his role of
a technician. Hupfer has definite opinions on many
musical questions, but as the Basement's major-domo
he rarely discusses anything except how pianos work.
Few pianists know much about the mechanics of a
piano, and Hupfer has found that by sticking to this
subject he gives them a calming sense of communing
with authority. The sight of the twenty pianos also
tends to steady his clients' nerves. To be sure, the
pianos represent only a fraction of the library's total
stock, and one or two of them may have already been
booked for the time in question, but twenty grand
pianos in one room look like a lot and it is easy for a
client to make himself believe that out of so many one
will prove just right. Most of Hupfer's clients find that
entering the Basement gives them a feeling of excitement, engendered to some extent perhaps by their
awareness that a Model D sells at retail for sixty-nine
hundred dollars* but more probably by their awareness that the room itself is famous among concert
pianists all over the world and that great musicians
have deliberated there over which Steinway to use,
and have played some of these very pianos on memo-
rable occasions. Almost all musicians, with the possible exception of a few of those who are recognized as
great themselves, derive a thrill from Hupfer's Basement and a feeling of security by association.

Sometimes Hupfer wishes the Basement didn't have
quite such a reputation. The fame of its former clients

---

*In percentage terms, the rise in the price of the Model D does not
compare with the rise in the price of clothbound picture books, but the
figure, as of 1977, still seems substantial. It is $14,500.

tempts some borrowers to anthropomorphize the older instruments, attributing to them the personalities of the celebrities who have played them. The piano with the library number CD-15, for instance, is widely known among regular borrowers as the Rachmaninoff, and a few of them believe that it has in some way acquired the spirit of that celebrated composer and pianist. Rachmaninoff did play CD-15 several times, and Hupfer concedes that it may possess an odd, mellow tone, but he is discouraged when he finds a client staring reverently at it as if half expecting it to bang into the C-Sharp-Minor Prelude all by itself. He does what he can to keep the process of selecting a piano on a businesslike basis, free from such supernatural snags. "When you come right down to it, old Rocky played on hundreds of other pianos," Hupfer says. "There's no sense getting spooky about it. My idea is that these pianos are just pianos, and if CD-15 sounds a little peculiar—well, it's probably just because she's getting old."

Hupfer's admission that CD-15 may have a tone of its own is not the only instance in which he, perhaps unconsciously, neutralizes his efforts to have people look upon his charges as interchangeable. From time to time, he succumbs to a certain affectionate regard he has for one or another of them. He will put his hand on a piano's case, like a man clapping an old friend on the shoulder, and ascribe to it an individuality that, according to his credo, it can't possess—one is "singing," another is "hard" or "brilliant," and a third he may even describe in moments of extreme affability as "a dog that sounds like a handful of dried bones." Hupfer has two principal helpers—Morris Schnaper, who tunes the Basement pianos, and George Shapiro, an assistant regulator. Schnaper is at least as forgetful as Hupfer of the fact that one piano is supposed to be just like another. He is often in the midst of a tuning job when a client arrives seeking Hupfer's services, obliging him to put aside his tools and wait until a decision has been reached. Schnaper likes nothing better at such times than to gossip in a helpful spirit about the pianos, especially if the client is an awe-struck newcomer bewildered by the multiplicity of choice. A small, middle-aged man with an inscrutable smile of wisdom, Schnaper has amassed a vast store of piano small talk in the thirty-seven years he has been tuning. He remembers the reviews of most of the important performances each instrument has appeared in, who has played it recently, and the compliments it has been paid by distinguished pianists. Although neither awe-struck nor a newcomer, Oscar Levant is one of the clients who love to hear this sort of thing. But since Schnaper's lore obviously and outrageously violates Hupfer's tenet that a piano should be judged on its objective merit, the tuner usually whispers his inside information to the client when Hupfer is apparently not listening. This makes even the most trivial of his items sound important—so important, in fact, that one young pianist to whom Schnaper hissed a piano's pedigree said later that he wasn't quite clear what its story was but that he got the general impression it must have been put together, bit by bit, by Catherine the Great.

Experience has proved to Hupfer's satisfaction that merit alone should be the criterion for choosing a piano. "If the artist himself doesn't hear that the instrument is right, he's practically sure to think, sometime before his concert, that he should have picked another," he says. "There's no other system that will work. But it's surprising what other systems are tried. A lot of the young ones just play the numbers. Somebody famous gives a recital, and afterward the stage is filled with people looking inside the piano, trying to see which number he uses. Or they will hear that So-and-So plays Number So-and-So, and that'll be the one they all want to borrow." Years ago, the Basement pianos were identified by the last three digits of their factory serial numbers, which gave borrowers an approximate idea of their comparative ages. When a borrower couldn't find a better basis for a choice, he often settled for the newest. This proved wearing both on the newest and on the staff, so the present library-number system was devised. The numbers are chosen arbitrarily, signify nothing about a piano's age, and are assigned at random; serial numbers are not engraved on Basement pianos until they are sold as used instruments or are otherwise retired from circulation. This device has pretty much put a stop to the scramble for new pianos, but the clients still fall far short of Hupfer's ideal. Not long ago, for instance, he had to temper his sympathy with skepticism when a young pianist came in and said he had been advised by Horowitz to borrow his piano—a story so unlikely that only a desperately nervous soul would dream of being caught with it. In Schnaper's opinion, such behavior should be understood, not condemned. "The artist is always erratic," he says. "He is sick with anxieties. Either he was born sick, and thus became a musician, or else he has trained himself up to sickness."

Hupfer's hold on the confidence of his clients depends above all, of course, on keeping the Basement

William Hupfer in the Basement of Steinway Hall attending to one of his charges.

Franz Mohr, now Steinway's chief tone regulator, surrounded by a few concert grands.

Scheer checks sales materials in the trunk of his car.

*Below:* George F. Scheer at his office desk in Chapel Hill, North Carolina.

pianos in superlative working order. In "The Care of Your Piano," an instruction manual that accompanies each new Steinway, it is suggested that for home use the instrument be tuned four times a year and its tone regulated "from time to time." The Basement pianos, on the other hand, are tuned and regulated almost continually; hardly has one been given a clean bill of health when its insides are laid bare again and another job of tuning and regulating it gets under way. Each piano is checked—and the appropriate corrections are made—after each of its concerts. An instrument scheduled to appear twice at, say, Carnegie Hall within a week is moved across the street to the Basement and back between dates so that Hupfer and his staff can go over it, like trainers going over a boxer between rounds. If a piano hangs around Steinway Hall for any length of time without being chosen by someone, it gets a routine examination to cure any ills that inactivity may have bred. As soon as one has been given the nod, it gets a going over before the pianist practices on it, another the day before the concert, and another an hour or so before curtain time, when it is in position onstage and beyond danger of unsettling jars, jolts, and sudden temperature changes. A piano that gets so much attention is unlikely to develop a serious defect, since symptoms of disintegration are almost sure to be caught and corrected in their early stages; most of the troubles discovered require only minor adjustments. One or two notes may be slightly out of tune, for example, but it never happens—as it does in some homes—that all the strings are down a tone in pitch and fouled up with Christmas-tree tinsel as well.

Nevertheless, after a piano has gone through some-

thing like fifty concerts—the exact number depends
upon who has been playing it and how many hours of
practicing on it have preceded its appearances—the
hammer felts, which are made of compressed lamb's
wool, inevitably begin to show signs of deterioration;
their repeated striking of the strings wears tiny
grooves into their surfaces, flattens their tips, and
hardens the felt itself. Since this has a bad effect on
tone, as soon as Hupfer detects the signs of hammer-
felt trouble in one of his pianos he retires the instrument temporarily from circulation and sets about re-
storing its felts to the proper grooveless, gently
rounded, and firm but not hard condition. A recent
job he did on CD-197, which both Brailowsky and
Rubinstein have played, was fairly typical. During the
preceding three months, it had been borrowed, in
quick succession, by Lélia Gousseau, Muriel Kerr
(twice), Doda Conrad, Walter Hautzig, Gina Ba-
chauer, Paul Badura-Skoda, Rosalyn Tureck, Anatole
Kitain, the Down Town Glee Club, the American
Broadcasting Company (twice), Monique de la Bru-
chollerie, and Walton High School. It was time,
Hupfer decided, for a complete checkup, which would
take the better part of a day and would include regulating the action, or mechanism, of the piano as well as
the condition of the felts on the hammers, which are
directly responsible for its tone. He ordered CD-197
rolled into the corner beside the bench under the
bright light. Action regulating is not as delicate an art
as tone regulating, and frequently Hupfer leaves it to
his assistants, but the two are closely related, and
when he has time, he is inclined to tackle them both.
He began by unfastening the top and leaning it against
the wall. Then, after examining the legs, the lyre (the

frame that holds the pedals), and the trap work (the pedals and their mechanism) to make sure that they were solidly attached and working smoothly, he unscrewed the key blocks at either end of the keyboard, took off the fall-board (the panel immediately above the keys, with "Steinway & Sons" stencilled on it in gold), and pulled out the entire action, keys and all, as if he were pulling a drawer all the way out of a bureau, and set it on his bench. It was easy to see that the hammer felts—all eighty-eight of them—were slightly grooved, those in the middle octaves, which get the hardest workout, a little more so than the rest. Hupfer picked up a small piece of coarse sandpaper attached to a wooden handle and began to file, or rub, down the felts, one at a time. In each case, it took only a few strokes—"a mere grazing," Hupfer calls it—to restore the proper surface; even so, the process can't be repeated more than about a dozen times before the hammers need re-covering at the factory. The problem confronting Hupfer was to eradicate the grooves without rubbing off any more felt than necessary and, in the same few motions, to achieve just the right degree of roundness in the shape of the hammer. (If a hammer is too flat, it will muffle the tone of its note; if it's too pointed, it will make the note sound tinny.) Furthermore, Hupfer had to make certain that in tinkering with the shapes of the felts he did not throw out of kilter their precise gradation—from the little hammers in the treble to the big ones in the bass; a man who wasn't sure of exactly what he was doing could ruin a set of felts with no more than half a dozen inept brushes of the sandpaper. Tuners are sometimes tempted to take a crack at filing hammers, because it looks so easy when it's done by an expert regulator.

Hupfer, who knows that even deep grooves are preferable to the mess an improperly trained tuner can make, has for the past several years lectured on regulating at the annual conventions of both the National Association of Piano Tuners and the American Society of Piano Tuner-Technicians, the two leading organizations in the field, and on each occasion has warned his audience that as far as the felts are concerned, the best policy for tyros is hands off.

After Hupfer had filed all the hammer felts, leaving them as clean and creamy white as brand-new tennis balls, he slid the action back into CD-197 and put it through a series of trials designed to make sure that all its six thousand parts were in good working order. Using a long stick with one slightly concave edge, he checked the alignment of the keys, which should be a trifle higher in the middle octaves than at the ends, and with several small lead weights he tested each key's balance, measuring the pressure to push it down and the force behind it as it rose back into place. Then he pulled up a piano bench, sat down, and, with his head bowed over CD-197 as he thoughtfully listened for the sound of a bad felt, began to play a tuneless series of notes with the second finger of his right hand, holding his wrist stiff; to the uninitiated, he might well have seemed a man who had not yet taken his first piano lesson, but Hupfer says that of all the techniques in his repertory, his stiff-wristed touch was the hardest to learn. A tone regulator must be able to play a series of notes in which each blow is precisely as hard as all the others; failing that, he will attribute tonal variations to the felts when in reality he himself is responsible for them. To complicate matters, the urge to do the reverse—to vary the stroke in order to make the tones even—is practically irresistible, especially to anyone who, like Hupfer, knows how to play. Hupfer thinks that Paderewski and Rachmaninoff, in protesting that their ears weren't acute enough to spot shadings in tonal quality, were mistaken; it was not the ear they lacked, he says, but the uncompromising rigidity of touch necessary to bring them out. His theory is that when either of them ran across a bad felt, he would become aware that something was wrong, but that upon replaying the note he was—fortunately, from a pianist's point of view, though not from a tone regulator's—led by the habits of a lifetime to make an unconscious correction in his touch.

As Hupfer's hand moved over CD-197's keys, he listened intently for the danger sounds—too much volume in a note or a trace of tonal deadness, both hinting at excessive hardness in the tip of its felt. He found several hammers whose tips were on the hard side, and each time he made a note with a piece of chalk—a small mark on the key-stop rail, which is a strip of wood that runs the length of the keyboard and helps keep the keys aligned. Regulators have a set of hieroglyphics, something like the symbols hoboes use, to indicate which felts are imperfect and in what respect. In this case, Hupfer's markings were for his own benefit, but if he had been suddenly called away, another tone regulator could have taken over without asking any questions. After Hupfer had located and marked all the bad tips—there were about ten of them —he pulled the action out a second time, put it on his bench, and began to make the needed repairs. A tone regulator corrects hardness in a tip by jabbing the felt with three ordinary sewing needles set in the handle of a shoemaker's awl. Two or three jabs, often, are enough. In making them, Hupfer is aware that he is diminishing a quality in a piano that many musicians admiringly call "brilliance"—volume, that is, created with a minimum of effort. But maximum volume means a lessening of resonance, and perfect resonance is the goal toward which Hupfer is constantly striving.

When the tips, or top felts, were all in order, Hupfer replaced the action and began plunking away at the keys again, this time listening for trouble in the under felts, in the interior of the striking part of the hammer. For perfect tone, a resilient top felt must be supported by a resilient under felt. "You listen for a kind of harshness," he says. "If the under felt is too hard, you'll get a clanging effect. It's not an easy thing to describe, but you might say it is a real nasty sound." The cure, again, is needle jabbing, but for under-felt work Hupfer uses a longer three-needle pick and delivers more forceful jabs, aimed far in toward the shoulders of the hammer. After tracking down all the under-felt trouble and making the appropriate marks, Hupfer hauled out the action once again and went to work on its hammers with his longer pick. Once he came across an exceptionally stubborn case, which refused to yield to his plunging jabs, and had to resort to the extreme measure of wiggling the needles about in the heart of the massed fibres. When the last of the ailing under felts had been coaxed into an acceptable state of resiliency, he smoothed down a little surface roughness he had caused here and there, and put CD-197 back together for the third and final time. The job was done. It had taken him a little over eight hours.

In view of the prolonged and painstaking labor that goes into regulating the tone of a piano, it grieves Hupfer to realize that many pianists share the inability, real or fancied, of Paderewski and Rachmaninoff to hear what he has achieved, and he is inclined to rank pianists by what he acknowledges is a rather special criterion—their sensitivity to hammer-felt conditions. He is consequently a great admirer of Frank Sheridan ("There is a man you can seldom, if ever, fool about tone"), and still talks wonderingly about a dazzling demonstration of aural acumen by Friedrich Gulda, the Austrian prodigy who a couple of years ago, at the age of twenty, made his United States début in Carnegie Hall. The Gulda concert got a good deal of advance publicity because the immigration authorities, acting under a strict interpretation of the Internal Security Act, held Gulda on Ellis Island for questioning until two days before he was to appear. When they were satisfied that having belonged to one of the Hitler Youth groups was something Gulda couldn't have helped, they released him and he hurried to the Basement, arriving there around four in the afternoon. He selected the second instrument he tried, and was left alone with it so that he could start practicing immediately. Steinway Hall closed down for the night and Hupfer went home, but the Basement was left open and Gulda continued to play until nearly midnight. Shortly after Hupfer arrived at work the following morning, the telephone near his workbench rang. It was Gulda, calling from his hotel; he loved the piano, he said, but he did feel that the F-sharp above high C needed regulating. "I didn't think it was possible," Hupfer said later. "I knew the boy had been through a tough time, and I figured there was no telling what he might be imagining. But, anyhow, I walked over and tried the note, just to be able to say I had. An amazing thing! He was absolutely correct!"

Facing the fact that for every Sheridan or Gulda there are a number of pianists who profess to feel that tone regulating is hardly worthwhile, Hupfer says, "Now, I will admit that the effect of the felts on tone is a small thing compared to all the other influences. Most of your tone, of course, is built right into the instrument. It's not just the sounding board but the entire piano, down to the smallest screw, that vibrates, and that's what sets up the sound waves. Even the stage of the concert hall vibrates with the piano, so you have to count that in, too. Well, the felts *are* just one part of the whole thing, but you can't do anything about all the rest of it unless you want to go out and start from the beginning and build yourself a completely new piano. The felts are the one part you can change. When you look at it that way, they are very important. I wouldn't expect anybody but another piano man to know exactly what I do, or hear the tone exactly the way I hear it. But when an artist doesn't hear it at all—that seems pretty funny." One case Hupfer considers pretty funny involved a library piano stationed at Worcester, Massachusetts. There had been continuing complaints about it, despite the fact that Hupfer had gone up there twice to inspect it and both times had found its tone to be wholly in conformity with the ideal. One particular pianist, it developed, had become antagonistic to the piano and had established a local vogue for saying derogatory things about it. Hupfer finally brought the Worcester piano back to New York and sent a substitute up to take its place. The complaints ceased, but Hupfer was left with a piano no one would want—no one, at least, who knew its reputation. He mulled this situation over for a while—as he saw it, an injustice was being done to an innocent piano—and then, like a thief changing the plates on a hot car, he assigned the instrument a new library number and set it out on display in the Basement. Within a matter of weeks, the pianist who had ruined its good name came in to pick an instrument for a Carnegie Hall recital. He picked the Worcester piano as his favorite of the lot.

Happily, however, quite a few people besides Sheridan and Gulda appreciate Hupfer's workmanship. Greiner hears what Hupfer does to a piano's tone. So do all seven members of the Steinway family now active in the business—from Theodore E., the president, down to Frederick, a young production engineer. So do hundreds of concert pianists and at least a couple of music critics. That is to say, all these people can agree, within limits, on whether the tone of a note is right or wrong and can discuss, in a loose way, why. When it is right, they describe it with adjectives like "true," "clear," "bright," "singing," and "alive"; they say that "it sounds as if it might go on forever," even though they know piano notes begin to disintegrate as soon as they have been struck. Shapiro can do more than that. After four years' intensive study under Hupfer's direction, he can adjust the felts of a piano until they produce the ideal tone as he hears it, and nine times out of ten Hupfer will announce that it sounds ideal to him, too. Shapiro, a former G.I., joined Steinway & Sons in 1946 and, after a period of training, was assigned to the company's Retail Department, where he tuned new pianos before they were delivered and checked rented pianos before they were sent out and upon their return. Presently, word got around that he might have the makings of a tone regulator. Such a find is a big event around the Steinway premises, and Hupfer snapped him up and taught him the finer points of how to jab felt. Nowadays, Shapiro has no trouble with any aspect of his work except the question of the final jab or two. "All I need to do is check over what he does, and I suppose even that isn't necessary any more," Hupfer says. "When I hear something that Shapiro hasn't heard, it's a pretty small thing. It's never what you could call wrong. Just something a little less than perfect. I point it out and he agrees and we give it another touch and then it's right."

Hupfer has been interested in the piano, if not in piano work, for as long as he can remember. His father, Edward Hupfer, was a piano-factory workman who, although he spent the better part of his adult life with Steinway, also put in several years with other piano manufacturers in the metropolitan area; he was employed by Krakauer Brothers at the time William was born, in the Bronx in 1896. William and his brother Walter, two years his junior, went to P.S. 29, on Cypress Avenue in the Bronx, where neither boy showed much enthusiasm for study. Walter, who is now a senior member of the Outside Tuning Staff, which is primarily concerned with tuning privately owned pianos, liked baseball. William was interested in playing the piano. He took lessons for five years, and while he displayed some talent, he gave no indication of having a singularly keen ear for tonal niceties. When he got his job with the dance orchestra, during the summer before his senior year in Morris High

School, in the Bronx, he found making money so exciting that he was reluctant to return to his classes in the fall. He consulted his father about the idea of quitting school and going to work. "I think you ought to make up your mind one way or the other," the elder Hupfer told him. With this impeccable advice to guide him, William looked for a job. There appeared to be nothing in sight for a fair-to-middling seventeen-year-old piano player. In view of the senior Hupfer's profession, a piano factory would have been a logical second choice, except that he felt he would be embarrassed by the taint of nepotism, however slight. He got a job as runner for a Wall Street brokerage house, but a few weeks of that so softened his morale that when his father, who was then working in the old Christman Piano Company's plant in the Bronx, offered to recommend him to the foreman there, he was ready to forget his fancy principles and was taken on as a chipper—one who gives piano strings their first, crude tuning right after they have been installed. For a young man with Hupfer's ear, chipping proved a cinch, and before long he advanced to preliminary tuning. Word of his proficiency soon reached Steinway, and in 1917 he switched to Long Island City as a tuner.

In 1925, after Hupfer had spent seven years in the Steinway factory (and a year in the Army), the firm transferred him to Manhattan to learn general repair work, and even some regulating, in preparation for going out with pianists on the concert circuit. At that time, any pianist of major rank took at least one piano and a piano man with him when he went on tour. Hupfer's first trips were with, successively, Rudolph Ganz, Myra Hess, and Yolanda Mérö-Irion. In 1928,

Rachmaninoff had trouble of some sort with his travelling tuner and appealed to Greiner to help him find a replacement. Greiner suggested Hupfer. Rachmaninoff was worried by Hupfer's comparative lack of experience. "Just try him," Greiner said. "You don't have to marry him. If you don't like him, we'll find somebody else." The trial took place in Montreal. When they reached that city, Rachmaninoff said to Hupfer, "Let me know when the piano is ready." Hupfer went to the concert hall, sweated over the instrument for some time, and then, fearing the worst, called up Rachmaninoff at his hotel and told him that he thought it was all right. Rachmaninoff went right over, sat down, and played a few bars. "Then he got up and he said, 'That's fine,' " Hupfer recalls. "I couldn't tell anything from his face. That's all he said. I didn't know whether he meant it was good or great —or just lousy." Hupfer was in suspense until about a week later, when, after additional concerts in two other cities, he and Rachmaninoff returned to New York and Rachmaninoff conferred with Greiner. "I went into Greiner's office afterward," Hupfer says. "I saw right away that he was all smiles, so I knew Rachmaninoff had said I was going to be all right. Greiner had been worried about it, because as far as he was concerned there was nothing too good for old Rocky." For the next thirteen years Rachmaninoff took Hupfer with him whenever he went on tour. He never again bothered to check Hupfer's work before a recital, and he never complained about it after one.

While Hupfer was on tour with Rachmaninoff, his first chore upon arriving in a city—usually in the morning—was to persuade the local Steinway dealer to send a practice piano up to Rachmaninoff's hotel room. That was not difficult, for the dealer knew that he could easily sell any piano Rachmaninoff had used. Rachmaninoff didn't care how the practice piano sounded. All he wanted was a keyboard on which he could keep his fingers limber, but he invariably showed his appreciation of the dealer's cooperation by autographing the instrument when he was through with it. This accounts for the fact that today there are hundreds of Rachmaninoff's "personal" pianos all over the country, and helps explain Hupfer's disgust when Basement patrons grow romantic about CD-15. Once the practice piano had been arranged for, Hupfer would stroll over to the concert hall to make sure Rachmaninoff's own piano had arrived. He would tune it and make whatever other adjustments might be needed as a result of rough handling in transit, and by noon he would be finished, and have nothing to occupy him until it was time for the evening performance. "I never knew what to do with myself," he recalls. "I ate lunch as slowly as I could. I went to the movies whenever there was one I hadn't already seen. I read every magazine and newspaper I could find, and I'm sorry now that I didn't have a taste for books—I could be an expert on pretty nearly everything. It was a dreadful life for a young man. I had to fight temptation every afternoon." Hupfer generally ate dinner with the Rachmaninoffs in their hotel suite. (The pianist's wife, Natalie Satin, always went on tour with her husband.) The meal over, Hupfer would get a taxi, escort Rachmaninoff to the hall, and stand by in the wings until the last note of the last encore had been played. The theory was that if anything went wrong with the piano, Hupfer could leap out and repair it. "It was a pretty funny idea," Hupfer says. "I figure old

Rocky must have picked it up somewhere in Europe, where a piano might need retuning during the intermission, or break a hammer, or something of the sort. But these old babies of ours are built to last, so nothing like that ever happened. I was always standing there ready, for all those years, and I never had a thing to do except listen."

Ten years ago, the war and the rise in piano-transportation costs ended the era of the personal tuner, and Hupfer did not regret its passing. Right from the start, he liked his stationary assignment in the Basement, and the fact that when he was tinkering with pianos he never had a dull moment in the afternoon. He was promoted to chief of the Basement one evening in 1946 after Greiner took him to his home for dinner. Hupfer's predecessor, Messerschmitt, had decided to leave Steinway, but Hupfer hadn't been told about it. While Greiner knew that in many ways Hupfer would be a fine choice for the post, he wasn't sure he could handle the tone-regulating part of the job. After coffee, he asked Hupfer to take a look at one of his two Steinways and see what he thought of it. The piano was in terrible shape and Hupfer said so, describing precisely what was the matter with its felts and how they would have to be fixed. All this tallied exactly with what Greiner knew about the piano, and without any further preliminaries he offered the position to Hupfer, who immediately accepted it.

After work, Hupfer often goes to a concert, accompanied by his wife, who is also a native of the Bronx and who was a film cutter for a motion-picture studio in Fort Lee, New Jersey, when he married her, in 1919. There is sometimes an element of business in these

evenings, because Hupfer feels it never does any harm
to hear his clients perform, so he can sound agreeably
informed the next time they come in, but for the most
part he goes to concerts simply because he likes music.
As a member of the audience, he pays no attention to
the piano's tone, even if he has been working on it all
day. "What I can do to the tone is nothing compared
to what the pianist does," he says. "And after hours
I'm only interested in that." He likes piano recitals
best, orchestral programs next best, and operas least.
"I am so used to working with one tone at a time that
the full range of a big ensemble seems too spread
around" is his explanation. Apart from going to concerts and playing the piano at home, Hupfer's recrea-
tions are pretty much confined to baseball (he is
strictly a Yankee man) and his automobile, currently a
1952 Oldsmobile 88. He doesn't like to drive the car
as much as he likes to tinker with it. "I don't know why
it is, but I love to make sure that every last one of the
gadgets on it is in perfect working order," he says. "I
like to think that mechanically it couldn't be in better
shape."

In 1891, Paderewski borrowed a Steinway from
Steinway Hall, which was then on Fourteenth Street,
opposite Lüchow's, for his first American concert
tour. He thought it took too much effort to push down
its keys. "I immediately complained of this fault to the
Steinways and they said it would be changed at once,"
he wrote years later, in his "Memoirs." "But it was *not*
changed, because the workmen refused to accept my
criticism. Every one of those workmen, the regulators
especially, was an expert and an authority in his own
way. They were convinced that what they were doing

must be accepted as perfection; that they had not to adapt themselves to the wishes of a mere artist, but that the artist should adapt himself to the piano. They respected my criticism—and ignored it." Hupfer takes much the same attitude toward the wishes of the artists, mere or otherwise, with whom he deals, but it might be more accurate to say that while he, too, respects their criticism, he puts up with it rather than ignores it. Not long ago, he was in the Basement when a young girl pianist who has made quite a splash in concert circles during the past few seasons came in to pick a piano for a recital she was about to give at Town Hall. After an exchange of greetings, she looked around at the pianos. "Goodness!" she said. "It always surprises me what a lot of them there are. You know so much more about them than I do, Mr. Hupfer. Tell me, which one do you think is the best for me?"

"That's a hard question for me to answer," Hupfer assured her gravely. "We have quite a few pianos and they're all pretty good." He lifted the top of the nearest Model D and rolled up a bench. "Now, here's one I think you might like," he said.

The young lady sat down at it, played a few chords, and shook her head. "It's not brilliant enough," she said. "And I'd prefer one with a lighter action."

Hupfer nodded sympathetically and led the way to another Model D, which, after several moments of what looked like solemn deliberation, he had selected at random.

Again the young lady struck a few chords. "Oh, this one is awfully good," she said. "But if I could just find one with a shade more brilliance." Gamely, Hupfer pointed out a third and a fourth, and a quarter of an hour later the young lady was sitting at the piano she had first tried. She played it for some time and then said, "I like this one very much. It may not be *quite* as brilliant as I wanted, but there is something about the tone. It has a certain quality to it—a kind of substance, you might say. And the action is just right." She stopped playing, and added, "Yes, I believe I'll take this one."

"It's a good piano," Hupfer said.

"I guess, now that I come to think of it, it's the first one you suggested," the young lady said.

Hupfer smiled, and made no comment.

\*

The Steinway Piano Company is now owned by the Columbia Broadcasting System, but I stopped by the Basement a few months ago and found it almost unchanged. The floor is new, but it is made of wooden parquet blocks exactly like the old floor—nothing less could stand the weight of the concert grands as they are rolled in and out to concerts and back. Since 1964, Mr. David W. Rubin has been head of the Concert and Artist Department, taking Mr. Greiner's place; and Mr. Franz Mohr, who received most of his training in Germany, is the chief tone regulator. Hupfer spotted Mohr when Mohr was working in the Outside Tuning Department as a tuner, and made him an assistant tone regulator. As for Hupfer, who is 80, he remarried not long ago, after his first wife's death. He retired, and then went back to work, and then retired again, but he still works regularly on a contract basis for the company, most often when the concert season is at its mid-winter peak. Hupfer is happy, full of vitality, and not in the least worried about the safekeeping of proper Steinway tone. Hupfer is confident that Mohr, his protégé, hears it exactly right.

CHAPTER 5

# Book Traveller
### GEORGE F. SCHEER

THERE are about two hundred American firms that publish what are called "trade books" —not textbooks or reference books but fiction, poetry, drama, biography, belles lettres, history, philosophy, books on contemporary affairs, children's books, and books that may not fit into any of those categories but also are meant to be read by literate people who like to *read* books. Not all trade books are literature, but every book that is or that aspires to be literature—as are, say, "Sense and Sensibility," "Alice in Wonderland," and "The Decline and Fall of the Roman Empire"—is a trade book. With uncharacteristic unanimity, trade-book publishers agree on the overriding importance of one question: How is one to transfer finished books from the warehouse to the hands of book buyers—people interested enough and affluent enough to pay for them? The trade-book publishers confront other serious problems: the cost of

printing and binding books (either in hardcover or
what are known as "quality paperback" editions)
keeps getting higher; topnotch editors are scarce; authors have no more respect for deadlines than they
ever had; and book reviews and free publicity for
books are harder to come by than they once were. Still,
book distribution seems more baffling than any of
these.

Trade-book publishing is a small specialty in an industry that itself is not very big. In 1972, the wholesale
value of all the books of all kinds that were sold in this
country was a little more than three billion dollars.
Even though this sum was twice as much as the book
publishers had received a decade earlier, the sales of
the book-publishing industry as a whole were nevertheless only slightly more than the sales of one soap
company, Procter & Gamble.* And three-quarters of
the money was earned by books that were not trade
books. Thirty per cent came from the sale of, among
other items, textbooks and standardized tests in book
form (nine hundred million dollars); twenty per cent
came from encyclopedias and other subscription reference books, mostly sold door to door (six hundred
and six million dollars); twelve per cent was professional and technical books for lawyers, doctors, scien-
tists, engineers, and others (three hundred and fifty
million dollars); four per cent was Bibles and other
religious books (a hundred and twenty-six million dollars); and mass-market paperbacks, which are counted
separately from quality paperbacks because they are

---

*In 1977, the wholesale value of books sales had increased to a little more
than four billion dollars; and, luckily for my comparison, so had Procter
& Gamble's sales.

distributed differently, more or less like magazines, accounted for eight per cent (two hundred and fifty-three million dollars). Trade-book sales were about seven hundred and fifty million dollars, and something like three hundred and four million of this came in through the book clubs. The remaining four hundred and forty-six million dollars covered sales of hardbound adult trade books, with a wholesale value of two hundred and forty-three million; quality paperbacks, worth fifty-five million; children's books retailing for a dollar or more, worth a hundred and twenty-eight million; and, finally, about twenty million dollars' worth of university-press books that were of general rather than specialized scholarly interest and were sold through trade channels. All of this represented the difficult part of book distribution. A good number of these sales were made to the country's libraries, but most of the books were sold to people through bookstores and the book departments of department stores.

The trade-book publishers' strong suit is variety. New tradebook titles—hardcover and quality paperback—average about twenty-seven thousand a year, or seventy-four a day. The *Times* gets nearly twenty thousand a year, or fifty-five a day, for review, although it cannot mention more than about twenty-five hundred. *Publishers Weekly*, the industry's trade magazine, divided the 1972 grand total of some thirty-eight thousand new books—new titles and new editions of old books, both paperback and hardbound—into twenty-three broad categories.

Books in the category that *Publishers Weekly* calls "sociology and economics," including texts and reference books, were by far the most numerous—more than

sixty-four hundred. Adult fiction—thirty-two hundred
—was second. Juveniles (fiction and nonfiction combined), science, and literature (essays, criticism, and
literary works considered classics) were tied, at
twenty-five hundred in each category. On down, in
dwindling order, came biography, medicine, religion,
and history, at fifteen hundred titles or more apiece;
poetry and drama (which were lumped together), art,
technology, education, philosophy and psychology
(another combination), travel, and general works, all
more than a thousand; sports and recreation, law,
business, home economics, language, music, and agri-
culture (three hundred and ninety titles for the last).
The number of new titles, omitting new editions, has
been growing since the Depression, from seventy-five
hundred in 1932 to twenty-six thousand four hundred
in 1972, but that tremendous increase is mostly in the
nonliterary categories, the leader being sociology and
economics. New books of adult fiction—novels and
short stories—were about as numerous then as they
are now. Biography and poetry and drama are up, but
by only a few hundred. Literature is up by more than
eight hundred. And almost any trade publisher would
admit that if he were to find a distinguished manuscript in any category—a candidate, let's say, for a
National Book Award—he would not be certain that
he could sell ten thousand copies of it.

Nobody I have ever met knows or cares more about
trade-book distribution than George Fabian Scheer,
of Chapel Hill, North Carolina, who is not a publisher
but a publisher's commissioned representative—a
travelling book salesman. Scheer's territory is the
South and Southwest, and he has been selling books

there for twenty-eight years, calling on individual bookstores, the book departments of department stores, and book wholesalers, or "jobbers." Scheer has a reputation as a wizard among book salesmen, and his colleagues also consider him unusually knowledgeable about many other aspects of publishing— for good reason, since Scheer sees the industry from several points of view. Although, in the course of two major and several minor selling trips annually, he is on the road between Richmond, Virginia, and Amarillo, Texas, as many as twenty-two weeks a year, and preparations for his travels take up most of his time for four or five months, and although when he isn't travelling he works for some hours every day as a liaison between publishers and booksellers, he is far from being just a book salesman. He is a historian (co-author, with Hugh F. Rankin, of "Rebels and Redcoats," a documentary account of the American Revolution), a writer of children's books ("Yankee Doodle Boy" and "Cherokee Animal Tales"), an editor (of the Meridian Documents of American History series, for World Publishing Company), and a book reviewer (for the old *Saturday Review,* the *Times Book Review,* and scholarly journals). Moreover, as a publishing consultant, he has advised, among others, the Child Study Association, Dow Jones & Company, the North Carolina Diabetes Association, the National Park Service, and the Smithsonian Institution. And he is a literary agent for a number of authors whose work especially interests him. Beyond his professional involvement with books, reading is Scheer's hobby. "I must admit that I have ruined myself as a serious reader," Scheer once said. "I have become a book-taster by force of circumstance, and I have to make a conscious effort to keep from rushing ahead—skimming, with too much curiosity, faster than I can read. I love to lose myself in a book—that's what I mean by 'serious' reading. But then I also enjoy mere tasting to an inordinate degree. I even get a thrill out of holding a well-made book in my hands, just from the way it feels. I suppose that explains how I got into all this to begin with."

I first met Scheer three years ago, in New York, at a meeting of the Society of American Historians, where I had a chance to tell him how much I liked "Private Yankee Doodle," a Revolutionary War memoir by Private Joseph Plumb Martin, first published in 1830, which Scheer had edited and annotated for Little, Brown. Scheer is a compact man in his middle fifties, who stands up straight with his shoulders back. He has a full head of close-cut black hair, graying at the temples; a trim salt-and-pepper mustache; and a full face, with round cheeks that come close to dimpling when he smiles. He speaks slowly and thoughtfully, with a faint trace of a Virginia accent. His manner is an attractive mixture of courtliness and friendliness. Our talk turned to book sales—rather naturally, since the room was full of authors—and I soon realized that Scheer knew more about the subject than the average historian. During the discussion, he offered no panacea, but he did observe that the trade-book publishers' distribution problems would get worse unless they did something practical to help old-fashioned, but not necessarily musty, independent local bookstores. Scheer has an economic prejudice in favor of such stores, since they make up two-thirds of his three hundred accounts, which buy for more than four hundred outlets, but his interest is also literary, emotional, and personal. He sees that many stores are struggling to survive, and fears that if the personal bookstores disappear—leaving only mail-order (including the book clubs), the chain bookstores, the mass-market-paperback racks, the department stores, the coin-operated book-vending machines, and the damaged- and remaindered-book outlets—literary quality will suffer. It will be harder for people to find the kinds of books he likes to read. "I like both fiction and nonfiction, and I guess I am sort of a nut about American history. The books I most enjoy usually fail to make the best-seller lists," Scheer told me. "They are seldom book-club selections—not of the major book clubs, anyhow. I really fear that if the personal bookstores diminish in size and number, the publishers will have to stop publishing what I like best. There will be no way to distribute a modest success—a book selling fewer than fifteen or twenty thousand copies. That is not enough to interest chain bookstores or department stores, which are both important to books of wide general appeal but try to concentrate, as far as they can, on fast-moving merchandise. You can't publish trade books for their library sales, which are not much more than ten per cent at best. Selling by mail, except on the vast scale of the big book clubs, is highly problematical. The personal bookstores are the only other way. Thank goodness they have not yet vanished. By some miracle, people—lots of them young people—keep on opening bookstores. You can almost take it for granted that the ventures are under-capitalized—that's the most common mistake. And most of these people are shocked to discover that running a bookstore is extremely hard work. However, if the bookseller does everything exactly as it should be done, and if the store is in the right place, it is possible

for him to do moderately well. So I do not say that all
is lost. But I have been watching booksellers, of all
ages, for more than a quarter of a century, and I've
seen that merely staying in business has steadily
grown more difficult. The personal bookstore cannot
thrive on best-sellers alone. It cannot do without
them, but it has to go well beyond the best-seller lists,
because it must attract what I call real book buyers.
These are the people who buy books constantly for
themselves—books they intend to read and keep.
There are people who cannot imagine getting through
life without a lot of books. They are like opera addicts,
who will skip a meal rather than miss a good performance. They are quite different from occasional book
buyers, who come in, once in a long while, to buy
'Jonathan Livingston Seagull,' because everybody is
talking about it, or a cookbook, because its author has
been interviewed on television that morning. Or a
book to give as a present. Some people are happy to
spend twenty-five dollars on an art book for Aunt Eliza
for Christmas although they never spend a nickel on
a book for themselves. The occasional buyer's money,
of course, is as good as the real book buyer's, and
there is scarcely a neighborhood where real book buyers alone could support a bookstore. Still, I am convinced that an independent bookstore cannot afford to
alienate those hard-core readers. They are difficult
and demanding, goodness knows. If one comes in for
the first time and asks for Kafka's 'Complete Stories'
and you don't have it, he may be willing to let you
order it for him. If he comes in nine days later and asks
for something else and you don't have *it,* he'll wonder
why not, out loud. Booksellers often answer, 'I'm
afraid we're sold out'—because they'd rather fib than

admit they haven't ordered the book at all. Maybe the customer believes it, maybe not. Then, four days after that, he comes in for John Kenneth Galbraith's new book and you don't have it. Well, you have lost that customer—probably forever. What's the use, he thinks. This store is hopeless. It doesn't have any stock worth mentioning. And he will look for another place, even if you are the only bookstore for miles."

Scheer shook his head. "The right balance is hard to achieve. The bookstore must satisfy a number of separate groups of people, and what pleases one group may not interest the other groups. There will never be a way of making books uniformly acceptable, so a broad inventory is most important. And yet the bookseller, since he has a limited amount of money to put into his stock, must also be able to guess what the whimsical, impulsive, occasional public for best-sellers is going to want large quantities of—and he has to make those guesses and order the books long before the public ever hears of them. Most bookstores are weeks away from the publishers' warehouses and cannot afford to wait until the answers are in. That's a hard job, when you think of the thousands of possibilities. How could you have anticipated 'Bury My Heart at Wounded Knee'?"

Scheer pointed out to me that running a bookstore in New York City is very different from running a bookstore in, say, San Antonio. "I don't mean that a New York City bookstore is easy," he said. "If it were, there would be many more bookstores in the city, and there would not be so many of them clustered in one ten-block stretch in midtown Manhattan. But New York booksellers are spoiled. The publishers are right around the corner. There are big jobbers right in New

York. The stores can demand delivery the following day and get it. But there are a lot of stores that sell books—perhaps three thousand—outside Manhattan. There are quite a few new jobbers around the country, but still many of those stores consider themselves lucky if they get books within a month or six weeks."

I saw Scheer in New York several times during the following couple of years, and then, at his suggestion, I joined him in New Orleans on one of his two major annual trips, to see what selling books was like. Scheer was well into his trip, having already covered Chapel Hill, Richmond, Nashville, and Atlanta. He met me at the New Orleans International Airport at noon on a warm and brilliantly clear Sunday. He looked fresh and jaunty in a tan open-necked sports shirt and tan summer slacks. I could hardly believe him when he told me he had had only a few hours' sleep. He had been caught in a bad rainstorm the night before, on the road from Atlanta, he said, and made an un-planned stop for the night, and then rose at the crack of dawn to finish the drive to New Orleans before my plane landed. "It wasn't anything," Scheer assured me. "When you travel as much as I do, you *count* on surprise delays, and I am just glad I had sense enough to stop for the night. Anyhow, Sunday is not a selling day. I use Sundays to catch up on paperwork, and I attempt to arrange my itinerary so that the long drives fall on Sundays. I ought to finish up New Orleans by Tuesday night—or Wednesday morning at the latest. The sad truth is that New Orleans, which used to be a fairly good book town, has been deteriorating. It may come back. There are all sorts of plans for civic revival in the air—a lot of rebuilding and renewal. I hope so, of course. I remember when I could not get out of New Orleans in much less than four or five days."

We were approaching downtown New Orleans, driving down Tulane Avenue, and Scheer pulled in at a motel. "I hope this is going to be all right," he said. "I've never stayed here before. Most unusual, because as a rule I stay at the same motels year after year—unless they start to come apart, as sometimes happens. I don't need anything very luxurious, so I hardly ever stop at a 'resort' motel, where I would have to pay ten or fifteen dollars more for essentially the same room. I've stayed for a long time at a nice place not far from the airport, but last trip the air-conditioner was broken, the plumbing was stuck, and there was nobody around who could fix anything, and I decided that that was enough." We checked in, after Scheer had looked over our rooms with a practiced eye and pronounced them sound. We partly unpacked the trunk of his car, a light-tan four-door Cadillac, taking out his suitcase and mine, a rotary address file, a portable electric typewriter, and his garment bag. We left his two big briefcases in the trunk.

The back seat and floor of the car were filled with cardboard cartons of what I later learned were bundles of publishers' catalogues with order forms tucked inside them. As a commission man, Scheer works for anywhere from eight to twelve different publishers at a time, and he sells more imprints than that, because some publishers distribute books for other houses. Since most of the big publishers have their own salaried salesmen, Scheer, like all other commission men, represents medium-sized and small houses. On this particular trip, he was selling for Hawthorn Books,

Schocken Books, Horizon Press, Pitman Publishing
Corporation, Stephen Greene Press, John F. Blair,
Louisiana State University Press, Holiday House,
Barre Publishers (which distributed for the Imprint
Society and David R. Godine), and Henry Z. Walck,
Inc. (which was then distributing for Bradbury Press).
"If there's a big best-seller on any of the lists, I shall
be surprised," Scheer said. "But I've got some good
books—Hannah Senesh's 'Her Life and Diary,' Lanza
del Vasto's 'Return to the Source,' Irving Howe's 'Decline of the New,' in paperback for the first time. I've
got Harold Rosenberg's 'The De-Definition of Art,'
and a beautiful book of photographs, Edward S. Cur-
tis's fabulous pictures of the North American Indian.
Godine has a splendid edition of Walt Whitman's
'Specimen Days.' There's B. Liddell Hart's 'Why
Don't We Learn from History?'—I expect that may do
well—and, from the L.S.U. Press, 'The Changing Politics of the South,' by William Harvard. James Ahern,
who used to be chief of police in New Haven, has
written a thought-provoking book, 'Police in Trouble.'
Naturally, I have more cookbooks, gardening books,
and books on how to do everything—from investing in
the stock market to making wine—than anything else.
Some of them are excellent, if I do say so. I don't have
much fiction this time. 'Another World,' by James
Hanley, some science fiction, and—oh yes, a gothic
novel called 'The House Called Edenhythe,' by Nancy
Buckingham. I understand it is good, if you care for
gothic novels."

Instead of travelling on an expense account and
driving an automobile owned or leased by a publisher,
as a house salesman does, Scheer pays all his own
expenses. His commission rates, which are more or

less standard, vary from ten to twelve and a half per cent on sales to bookstores and book departments and from five to seven and a half per cent on sales to jobbers. Commissions are figured monthly on the total amounts of the bills that his publishers send out to his accounts: the books' list prices multiplied by the numbers of copies bought minus the buyers' discounts (which range from forty to forty-six per cent) minus the buyers' credits for books returned. That means that Scheer's monetary interest in the sale of one copy of a given book is slightly more than half that of the author. An author's royalties are usually from ten to twelve and a half or fifteen per cent of his book's retail price. On a ten-dollar book, which a bookstore buys for six dollars, the author is likely to get a dollar and Scheer sixty cents. And, of course, Scheer, instead of having just one book, or perhaps a handful of books, going for him, has all the books in print of all his publishers as potential money-makers. However, Scheer's expenses are high. His territory is too big for him to handle alone; were he to call on all three hundred of his accounts, he would hardly get back to Chapel Hill from one sales trip in time to start out on the next, and he would seldom see his wife, Genevieve, or their twenty-one-year-old son, George. And so for the past nine years Scheer's expenses have included the salary and expenses of an associate, Roger Foushee, who calls on about half the accounts. Foushee, who is in his middle thirties, is black-haired and bearded. He was a political-science graduate student at the University of North Carolina when Scheer found him and put him to work. Now Foushee spends every available minute when he is not working for George Scheer Associates working for the liberal wing of the

Democratic Party in North Carolina and participating
in Chapel Hill's civic affairs. Scheer is teaching Foushee everything he knows about selling books, and
Foushee is learning his lessons well.

Scheer looked at his wristwatch. "We have to have
some lunch," he said. "You can't come to New Orleans and not eat, you know. It's immoral. Let's see,
Sunday lunch. I know—we'll have the shrimp salad at
the Pontchartrain Hotel. It's really good. New Orleans
carries on about its food until you are ready to go out
of your mind, but some of it is delicious. Just let me
make a couple of telephone calls and we'll go. I'll see
if I can get Tess Crager at her home. I love Tess. She
has an amazing bookstore out in the Carrollton district, near Tulane University. It is called the Basement
Book Shop, but it isn't underground. It's in an old
rickety frame building, formerly a butcher shop—a
fabulous place. And Tess is a fabulous woman, a real
book person. She reads everything that interests her
and then she calls her charge-account customers and
tells them what she has for them. They can come
around and pick the books up or send their chauffeurs
for them. I wouldn't want to be in New Orleans ten
minutes without calling Tess."

Scheer made his calls—he got Mrs. Crager all right
—and over the Pontchartrain shrimp salad, which was
indeed excellent, he continued to brief me. "Roger
attends all my publishers' sales conferences with me—
they're mostly in New York, and bunched around early
December and early June—and then we go back to
Chapel Hill and do our preparatory work, which is the
one part of selling books I seldom enjoy. We make up
matching jacket-books—one for each of us. They are
big ring binders, nearly as big as the biggest coffee-

table book, and they are our prime selling tool, along with the publishers' catalogues for the upcoming season. We give each new title at least a page. Usually, we mount its dust jacket on a hinge, so the bookstore buyer can lift it up, read the flap copy, and look at the back of the jacket, too. We take one publisher after another, from front to back, and each publisher's books, within its section, are in the same order as the publisher's catalogue, so if the buyer feels like it he can follow along in the catalogues as we turn the pages of the jacket-book. So you can see how important a jacket is, even at this early stage. We sell with jackets, not books. We may carry one or two finished books as samples—or perhaps a dummy book with blank pages, or a few sample pages, if the physical format is a crucial part of the book—but that's all. In the case of children's picture books, where the illustrations *are* crucial, we carry folded and gathered sheets—the book itself, unbound, with its jacket but without its board covers. Then Roger and I make up bundles of the catalogues, with order forms, and snap them together with a rubber band. That's a bigger job than you might imagine—three hundred bundles, and a couple of dozen extras, because you never know when you'll come across a new bookstore. It's physically tiring, but greatly preferable to trying to collate them at the last minute in a driving rain in a parking lot. When I load all my sales material into my car, the stuff weighs at least four hundred pounds."

The total driving distance around Scheer's territory —his route combined with Foushee's—is about twelve thousand miles. Scheer handles Chapel Hill, Richmond, Nashville, Atlanta, and New Orleans, and then he makes a giant loop covering Baton Rouge, Beau-

mont, Houston, San Antonio, Austin, Dallas, Fort
Worth, Amarillo, Oklahoma City, Tulsa, Little Rock,
and points in between. Foushee stays east of the Mississippi River, seeing everybody Scheer does not, and
his farthest point from home is Key West, Florida.
Together they cover twelve states (Virginia, North
Carolina, South Carolina, Georgia, Florida, Arkansas,
Alabama, Mississippi, Louisiana, Texas, Oklahoma,
and Tennessee), with a combined population of fifty-
two and a half million people—slightly more than a
quarter of the nation. In this huge area, there are more
than four hundred places to buy a book, but Scheer
and Foushee do not call on all the chain bookstores—
many of which have their books bought for them nationally, including most of the Doubleday, Brentano,
Walden, B. Dalton, and Pickwick stores—or on some
very small stores. In the matter of smallness, though,
borderline cases worry Scheer; he prefers to err on the
side of optimism. "I know that time is my capital, and
I'm always a little behind schedule. But if I want to
stop, I stop. Once, when I was just starting out, I
remember, I stopped at a very small sporting-goods
store in South Carolina, which kept a small shelf of
sports and regional-interest titles. The proprietor—a
terribly brusque old gentleman—immediately said, 'I
don't need any more books. I have all that I can sell.'
Well, in my eagerness I pressed him a little. He was
adamant. After a minute or two, I zipped my briefcase
closed and started to walk out. He was outraged.
'Where are you going?' he called after me. 'You don't
need anything, so I'm on my way,' I said. 'Now, wait
a minute, young fellow,' he said. 'I did not say that you
couldn't sit here and drum me for a while.' I sat and
drummed him for a while—it must have been forty-

five minutes—and in the end he gave me a right good order."

Although Scheer's part of the South and Southwest, with twenty-five per cent of the nation's population, buys less than ten per cent of the trade books sold in the United States, he does not feel he travels in a cultural wasteland. "Sales per capita are not good, but I greatly prefer the territory to any other, and I've sold books in the East and the Midwest, too," he told me. "I guess most commission men, given a choice, would pick a territory that included New York, Los Angeles, or Chicago. Those territories are certainly the most remunerative. I think you have to go deeper than raw sales figures, and for me there are a lot of towns in the South and Southwest where bookselling is a pleasure. Houston, for instance, is a great book town, and it seems to get better every trip. Nashville and Atlanta are good. I like Richmond—that's an interesting town to sell. And San Antonio—I love working there. But, considering my territory from a strictly economic point of view, not my personal bias, coverage is exceedingly expensive—a man has to travel a long way to sell a book, and he consumes his profits as he goes. He literally eats them up in food—not to mention time, gasoline, automobile wear and tear, and motel accommodations. That bothers the publishers, and with reason. They cannot afford to ignore a potential ten per cent of their total trade sales—no one in any line of manufacturing could—but the trick is to realize those sales without spending too much money in the process." Scheer explained that a publisher with his own salesmen would have to commit himself to paying something like sixty thousand dollars a year in salaries and expenses for two men to cover the South and

Southwest, so unless a house is selling six hundred thousand dollars' worth of books in the territory, commission-man representation, at ten per cent of *achieved* sales, is a bargain. "That gives me a degree of security," Scheer said. "Only a handful of publishers are selling that many trade books in my territory. I'm needed. In fact, I've worked for more than seventy different publishers, and though that sounds as if I hadn't done well, I've been fired only a few times. I've represented several houses for long stretches of time. For instance, I sold Holiday House on one of my earliest trips, and I've still got it. I've been with Hawthorn for many years, and with Walck since it began, fourteen years ago. I like to think, though—especially when one of my many sales managers is grumbling at me—that if I lose one publisher I can find another."

What Scheer likes best about his territory is the people he sells to. The buyers he calls on, many of whom are the owners of the bookstores, are his friends. He has known some of them for ten or fifteen years, or even the entire twenty-eight years he has been travelling. He can be sure of seeing them only two or three times a year, but he meets some a fourth time at the annual convention of the American Booksellers Association; some drop in on him if they are anywhere near Chapel Hill when he is at home; and he talks frequently to many of them on the telephone between trips. He has been with them in spirit, if not in person, through business crises, marriages, the birth of children and grandchildren, divorces, bankruptcies, and store expansions. Scheer is an emotional man, and his passion for books is second only to his pleasure in people.

Scheer's familiarity with small-scale retailing started when he was young. His father, George Fabian Scheer, Sr., ran a small quality-jewelry store, which Scheer's grandfather had established in 1887, in downtown Richmond. George, Jr., the eldest of four children, was born in 1917, and he helped out in the store from the time he could be helpful. He became an expert on antique clocks—Scheer likes to boast that he is the only book salesman in the country who is a fully qualified clockmaker—but when he was a schoolboy his ambition was to be a newspaperman, like Douglas Southall Freeman, then the editor of the Richmond *News Leader*. And, indeed, Scheer's first published newspaper feature story was bought by Freeman, and ran in the *News Leader,* when Scheer was sixteen. The transaction showed something about Scheer's natural talent for selling, because the piece was really a school composition, which had been given a C instead of the A that Scheer felt it deserved. He took it down to the *News Leader* office at four o'clock in the morning—knowing that that was when Freeman began his incredibly prolific days of editorial writing, history writing, and radio broadcasting—and handed it to Freeman in person. Freeman was impressed, bought the piece, and printed it the following day.

During the next five years, while Scheer was attending high school and the University of Richmond, he wrote and sold many more feature stories, mostly on local history, and illustrated some with photographs he took himself, but he was forced to change his career plans when his father died, in 1939. Scheer's mother was faced with the problem of supporting three younger children—Betty, who was fourteen; Julian, twelve; and Charles, eleven—so George, at twenty-

two, became the breadwinner, going to work in the
jewelry store full time. Scheer already believed in careful husbandry of time. (He had been impressed by a
motto on Freeman's office wall, "Time is ireplacea-
ble," partly because it was misspelled.) It might be
possible, he thought, to write a biography in odd moments, and after he had closed the jewelry store for the
night he did research on Francis Marion, the American
Revolutionary War guerrilla fighter known as the
Swamp Fox. Scheer is still trying to find time to write
the book. His research is complete, however, and one
of the happy by-products of his study was meeting
Miss Genevieve Yost, the librarian of Colonial Williamsburg, one Friday in 1940. Williamsburg owns a
valuable collection of American Revolutionary War
material, and Miss Yost, seeing that Scheer was frantic
to finish reading a stack of documents, was kind
enough to keep the library open an extra hour. The
least Scheer could do in appreciation was to drive Miss
Yost home. Within a few months, they were engaged.

An old back injury made Scheer ineligible for the
armed forces, but in 1944 he got a civilian job at Camp
Lee, near Petersburg, Virginia, working in the Quar-
termaster General's Office. He wrote training and
field manuals. (Two of his assignments were "Cooking
Dehydrated Foods" and "The Loading of Special-Pur-
pose Ten-Ton Vehicles for Transcontinental Rail
Transportation.") He learned a lot about book—or, at
least, manual—production, and, urged on by a soldier
friend, he drove down to Chapel Hill as the war was
ending to see if he could get a job with the University
of North Carolina Press, then directed by W. T.
Couch. En route, Miss Yost read aloud to him everything that Couch had written—for periodicals like the

*American Scholar, Saturday Review,* and *Publishers Weekly*
—on university-press management, and Scheer
memorized much of it. Couch was astounded that a
young field-manual author should have such a keen,
intuitive grasp of the problems of a university press,
but there was only one job open—salesman. Scheer
had been thinking of a job as an editor. Still, he accepted, hoping that he would be able to switch over to
the editorial side when something opened up. His
starting salary was minuscule. Miss Yost found that
she could get a job at the University of North Carolina
library, and she took it. Assuming that by adding two
salaries together they could survive, George and
Genevieve were married, on April 20, 1945.

Couch did not believe in breaking in a new salesman
gently. He started Scheer off by sending him to New
York, with no guidance except a list of buyers' names
and addresses. "Listen to those people," Couch said.
"Don't try to tell them anything. You'll learn more by
listening than by talking, because they know quite a lot
and you know very little." Scheer was insulted at the
time; later on he realized that the advice was wise. The
University of North Carolina Press had a reputation
for publishing good trade books as well as academic
works, and Scheer had almost no difficulty in getting
to see the important buyers, including Joe Margolies,
at Brentano's; Morris Axelrod, at Doubleday; Igor
Kropotkin, at Scribner; Harold Williams, at the American News Company; and William Epstein, at Booka-
zine. "I am sure that I seemed unbelievably green, and
annoyingly overconfident," Scheer recalls. "But they
were tolerant. I *had* to listen to them. I did not know
how many copies anybody was expected to buy.
When they gave me the numbers, I wasn't sure

whether I ought to be happy or sad."

Scheer's greenness led him to one triumph. On his second trip to New York, he called on Lewis Gannett, then the senior book reviewer for the *Herald Tribune,* and told him he thought Gannett had made a mistake in overlooking one of the press's books—"Mexican Village," by Josephina Niggli. Gannett seemed surprised at finding a book salesman in his office, but he did not seem angry. Scheer told Gannett, "Some of the major reviewers have said some marvelous things about it." (Scheer was thinking of major reviewers in Atlanta and Chapel Hill.) Gannett thought he had probably handed the book to his wife, Ruth, for a preliminary reading, and he said he would try to remember to ask her about it. Two weeks later, a rave review by Gannett appeared, ending with "In a year of notably little distinguished fiction, 'Mexican Village' shines like a scarlet cactus in the desert. . . . The whole crop of 1945 best sellers seems thin and wan beside it." The sales of "Mexican Village," which had been slow, immediately picked up, and the book went on to do very well.

Not long afterward, Scheer won more celebrity than a fledging book salesman can expect by writing an article about his own experiences, entitled "New Adventures Selling Books," for *Publishers Weekly.* The appearance of his piece made Scheer feel, for the first time, that he really was a book salesman rather than a bookish young man waiting for an editorial opening. By the spring of 1946, he had been promoted to sales-and-advertising manager of the press, and he had commission men working for him in the Northeast, the Middle West, and California. He himself handled the South and Southwest, and he also called on the major jobbers and some of the big accounts in the other territories. Having acquired some feel for the marketplace, Scheer had no intention of losing it by sitting behind a desk. Within a few years, the press's sales volume had more than tripled. Scheer was delighted with his job but uneasy because he needed more money than the press was paying him, so he persuaded North Carolina to let him represent the Princeton University Press and the University of Chicago Press, on commission, when he travelled. North Carolina continued to pay Scheer's travel expenses, and he paid North Carolina a percentage of his extra earnings. He added publishers to his list from time to time, until by 1952 he was representing five houses in addition to the University of North Carolina Press, and he could not help noticing that he might soon be paying his employer in percentages from his commissions almost as much as his employer was paying him in salary. The idea of quitting to become a commission man pure and simple tempted Scheer—he thought he might be able to earn more in less time, and conceivably get back to doing some writing—but going off the North Carolina payroll was a terrifying prospect to a child of the Depression. Scheer had bought some land in Chapel Hill and wanted to build a house there, because he and his wife, enchanted by the place, were sure they would like to live there permanently. He brooded over the decision, trying to summon the courage to quit, until Genevieve telephoned one afternoon to tell him that her doctor said she was pregnant. Scheer was ecstatic, and, with perfect reverse logic, he told his boss, Lambert Davis, who had by then become director of the press, that he would be leaving in thirty days.

There were times, especially during his first year as
a self-employed commission man, when Scheer felt he
had made a mistake. One big best-seller could have
relieved his anxiety, but he had none. (Before long, he
was to earn six thousand dollars in a month selling
Boris Pasternak's "Doctor Zhivago" for Pantheon.
"Salesmen sound crass, I know, because they talk so
much about the 'blockbuster,' the 'really big book,'
and the 'runaway best-seller,'" Scheer said to me
once. "I suppose we are even worse than publishers.
You have to remember that we are all a little desperate, because literature doesn't support itself. And then
—a thought that has consoled me considerably—not
all best-sellers are junk.") Scheer's morale was sus-
tained through low moments because he was traveling
with a veteran commission book salesman, Ed Jervis,
of Greensboro, North Carolina, whose talent for making money was legend. Scheer had met Jervis in a
bookstore on one of his trips, and they liked each
other immediately. They were complete opposites. It
is unusual for commission men to travel together,
since they must compete in every town for the same
buyers' time and attention, but Scheer and Jervis over-
came that conflict (they took turns going to stores
first) as easily as they avoided arguing about politics
(Scheer was a Republican, Jervis a Democrat). It was
more important that Jervis liked to shave before he
showered, while Scheer preferred to shower first.
They made their last trip together in 1964, when Jervis
stopped covering the Southwest. Jervis taught Scheer,
by example, that a man could make a good living selling books with candor, and without ever urging a
bookstore to order one book more than he thought it
could sell. Scheer, himself a candid man, had hoped

that selling would not require him to exaggerate or deceive; Jervis's success was proof it did not.

From the Pontchartrain, Scheer and I drove northeast on St. Charles Avenue, toward the French Quarter. "There is a nice young fellow named Oscar Brisky down there," Scheer said. "He's struggling to get a bookstore going—second-hand books, mostly—and I don't think he wants to buy anything much, but I'd like to stop by just to say hello." As we rode along, Scheer continued to outline the elements of bookselling: "What Roger and I look for at the sales conferences, after the sales conferences, and sometimes, though I hate to admit it, for days after we have started to sell, is the proper 'handle' for each of the new books. We need a capsule description, the shorter the better, that puts the book in the most realistic light as far as potential bookstore sales are concerned. We hope that the sales conference will give it to us, ready-made—that the editor or the publisher or the sales manager, or whoever presents the book, will tell us what it is. He *tries* to. But I have attended more than five hundred sales conferences, and most of the time the salesmen are forced to work it out for themselves. We are not shy about asking for help. Time and time again, one of us interrupts to say, 'It's beautiful. I'm sure the book is as distinguished as you say. But what handle can we use?' Even experienced and sophisticated editors, sometimes, have not thought that far. Or they cannot envision what happens when the salesmen meet the bookstore buyers. 'Handle' is a blunt, philistine word—precisely why the salesmen use it. We are seldom expected to assign the book its rightful place in literature—although if you could honestly say, 'I've read the galleys, and this is the best book that has been written since the King James Bible,' that would be an excellent handle. Mostly, we need to explain why *this* cookbook, in the face of all the other cookbooks, deserves a place on the cookbook-collector's shelf. Or why this gothic novel is expected to sell even though the competition is so great."

Underselling is almost as bad as overselling, Scheer said, and a good handle protects the bookstore from ordering too few copies. It is also something that the bookseller can use, as long as the book is in stock, to explain to his customers why they ought to buy it. "Just to give you an example, I'm selling a book called 'Home Landscaping You Can Design Yourself,' by Irving Roberts." Scheer went on. "There are half a dozen do-it-yourself landscaping books. The reasonable question is: Why another? Well, the Roberts book is practical. He is an engineer, an important officer in a big company, and landscaping is his hobby. His approach to landscaping is precisely what you would expect. He doesn't waste any time describing the beauty of the azalea or the perfume of the honeysuckle. He gets right down to the working specifications. And there is the handle I have been using—'landscaping as a professional engineer would approach the subject.' That's why the book should sell, and the orders have been good."

Scheer spoke about the frustration a book salesman experiences when he has what he thinks is a good book but lacks an effective handle for it—when the publishing house is excited and the author is optimistic but the salesman is unable to get anything like the advance orders that the book deserves. "That's a nightmare," he said. "You *know* that your orders are too low, and you know it is your fault. Six months later, on your next trip, the buyers are going to accuse you of having slighted the book. A couple of years ago, when I was selling for Farrar, Straus & Giroux, that happened to a distinguished novel by a well-known author. As the first sales figures came in, they were absurdly low. It wasn't just me. *All* the salesmen were missing on the book, because none of us had the right handle. And Farrar, Straus—greatly to its credit—stopped us. The book was postponed a whole season, so the sales strategy could be rethought. The next time around, with the help of an expensive promotion piece—a special advance paperback edition, with a letter from the publisher as a front cover—the salesmen more than doubled the advance. But that is an unusual case."

We took a right on Canal Street, then a left onto Decatur Street, and continued northeast, past Jackson Square and the French Market. "After they have an idea of the book, most buyers want to know how much enthusiasm there is for it on the publisher's part," Scheer said. "How big a sale does the house anticipate? You hear so much about 'surprise best-sellers,' and then you see so much evidence, in the form of piles of remaindered books, of publishers' dashed hopes, that it is hard to realize that most publishers' predictions are reasonably accurate. The salesmen usually play a part in formulating such predictions. The initial print order is often not decided upon until the house gets their reactions. Somebody on the editorial staff, reviewing the sales conference, may say, 'I noticed that the salesmen didn't exactly catch fire. I wonder if we have been thinking too big.' The estimated advance sale, which is ordinarily broken down into a quota for each territory, may be reduced. Some publishers ask their salesmen to help set their own quotas. Bookstore buyers want to be clued in to the publisher's forecast, and the size of the first printing ordinarily tells the story. If it is big—fifteen thousand is big—I make a little note about that in the jacket-book. There is no need to tell the buyers that the publisher thinks a book's prospects are routine—in fact, it can be embarrassing. Let's say I have a first novel that the house adores. I love it, too, and I want to give it a good spread—that is, sell at least a few copies to as many of my accounts as will take it. Still, the first printing may be no more than five thousand copies—which is often correct for a first novel. Even if we sell them all—every single copy that's left after the review copies and the complimentary copies have gone out—the advertising and promotion outlays for the book are going to be negligible. Not much more than a thousand dollars, probably, by almost any rule of thumb. Enough to buy a couple of modest ads."

Scheer went on to name some of the early indicators of success—selection by a major book club, an important sale of prepublication rights to a magazine, a movie sale, a paperback sale. "If anything of the sort has happened to one of my books, I do not suppress the news. But you have to keep the big-time block-buster, and the publicity it engenders, in perspective. There are likely to be half a dozen a season—maybe twelve a year—and the chances are, to my regret, that I will not have one. Books do sell five hundred thousand copies, but I am concerned with alerting my accounts to any title that is going to sell, say, ten thousand. They should not pass it over. Roger and I ought to get an advance sale of at least six or seven hundred copies of such a book in the South and Southwest, which means we should average two or three copies everywhere we stop. If any unusual publicity has been arranged, I make a note of that, too, but I am selling so far ahead of the publication date that this seldom is a factor. Then, perhaps the author is a celebrity, talented at self-promotion, and a fifteen-city tour is being scheduled for him. I'd mention that, of course, if he was going to be within radio or television range of the bookstore's customers. Conceivably, the book has a good advance review or two. I would paste them into the jacket-book. In the case of the average book, the bookseller sells the book to the customer with little outside help. The customer learns the book exists when he or she comes upon it on the table reserved for new books, or when the proprietor of the shop mentions it: 'Did you notice that Wirt Williams has a new novel, "The Far Side"?' There are big and little bookstores, but even in a big one—say, Ted Brown's downtown store in Houston—the proprietor and the salespeople know many of their customers by name. In a small suburban shop, where most of the trade may be charge-account customers, a total stranger stopping in to buy a book can be a rarity. So when I get to Oklahoma City, four weeks from now, and offer a comprehensive history of American lighthouses, a bookstore buyer there will have a good idea of how many he can sell—he can very nearly name the customers. To make those sales, he must have a copy of the lighthouse book on hand when each of those prospective buyers comes in—the right stock at the right moment. Ultimately, a bookstore is what is within its four walls then and there. The buyer puts the stock there, and the quality of the store depends exactly on how well the buyer has bought. What I do is try to clarify the potential of my books for my buyers. I call it selling. It *is* selling, but it is a form of collaboration, too."

The building, on Esplanade Avenue, near Bourbon Street, where Scheer expected to find Brisky's Old Mint Book Shop was vacant, but there was a sign in the otherwise empty window. "Marvelous!" Scheer said. "He's moved to Royal Street. I told him last year that he'd never make it here, and 1036 Royal Street is a much better location. He's still a little to the east of the mainstream of the tourist traffic, but I imagine it's a big improvement."

Brisky's new shop had an attractive sign and a quaint, bay-windowed façade, freshly painted white, but its interior was a letdown. The place was lined with second-hand books, as drab as only second-hand books can look. The display tables were card tables. There were only a dozen or so new books on two of them, and in the gloom their pristine dust jackets shone like jewels. I felt we were at a rummage sale rather than in a bookstore. Brisky, a slender, worried-looking man in his late twenties, wearing gray flannels and a tweed jacket, seemed discouraged. He said, "This is better, but it's still very slow. I am beginning to get a small number of fairly steady customers, and that encourages me. Mostly, I am attracting browsers, and I find I am working ridiculously long hours. I may decide to go back to school."

Brisky's spirits seemed to rise as he talked to Scheer, though Scheer said little. Mostly, he listened. He did remark that one could not expect too much too fast, he agreed with Brisky that running a bookstore was indeed hard work, and he reminded Brisky of a point he had made six months earlier: that the Old Mint Book Shop needed "a more sharply defined character" to make the browsers feel that it was an authentic part of the French Quarter. Brisky had said when we first came in that he was more interested in reducing his inventory than in increasing it, but before long he began to wonder what Scheer had to sell. Scheer had not brought any of his sales materials, but finally, at Brisky's request, he walked the half block to his parked car, returned with his jacket-book, and opened it out on one of the card tables. "I'm afraid I haven't got much for you," Scheer said, "but we can flip through the book so you can see what there is."

That seemed to whet Brisky's appetite. Whenever Scheer flipped a page quickly, Brisky wanted to turn back to it—as if he suspected Scheer of concealing a book from him. Within half an hour, Brisky had ordered about twenty books—single copies, and two or three copies of about twelve titles—which would cost him perhaps fifty dollars at his forty-per-cent discount, and he seemed positively cheerful. Scheer left a bundle of catalogues and order forms, and three or four postage-paid self-addressed George Scheer Associates mailing labels. "Drop me a line if there's anything I can do," Scheer said. "And I'll stop by on my next trip."

That pleased Brisky, and I realized that Scheer's call had flattered him—it was a token both of interest and of faith. "Remember, it never pays to get discouraged too quickly," Scheer said to him as we left.

During the next two days, we had to rush to fit in all of Scheer's well-established accounts. Though I knew that we couldn't waste a minute—not if we were going to get to Baton Rouge before Tuesday midnight—

Scheer relaxed with the buyers as if he had all the time
in the world. In New Orleans, they were almost all
women: Rhoda Faust, at the Maple Street Book Shop;
Kay Archer, at the book department of Maison
Blanche, a downtown department store; Suzanne
Link, at Books Etc.; Zelda Soignier, at the Tulane
Book Store; Florence Henderson, at the Catholic
Book Store; and Tess Crager, at the Basement Book
Shop. Except for Miss Faust, who had just taken over
the Maple Street Book Shop from her mother, Scheer
knew them well. He called them by their first names,
and they called him George. All the stores except the
Maison Blanche book department were in the Carrollton neighborhood, within a few blocks of one another.
They were not far from the Tulane campus—and the
Tulane Book Store was right on it—but I gathered that
the Maple Street Book Shop, which had a lot of paperbacks that might have been "suggested further reading," was the only store besides the Tulane Book
Store that was getting many college-student customers. Carrollton Avenue is a shopping and residential
street that runs through several well-to-do neighbor-
hoods. Books are luxuries, and bookshops go where
the money is. The bookshops in the Carrollton area
were attractive: though they were all small, with limited stock, each had a well-defined individual character. I thought how welcome any one of them would be
in my section of the West Side of Manhattan, where
hardcover books are difficult to come by. My favorite
was Tess Crager's high-ceilinged place, which had a
genial atmosphere of barely controlled clutter, its
walls adorned with scores of old photographs of literary celebrities—such as Hendrik Willem van Loon,
Gertrude Stein, Sinclair Lewis, W. H. Auden, Ogden

Nash—who had visited the Basement Book Shop. It was clear to me, though, why Scheer was gloomy about New Orleans as a book town. We had called on a major part of the city's bookstores, omitting only a couple of chain bookstores and the book department of the D. H. Holmes department store, whose buyer was out of town, but none of the orders was anything to boast about. Their total value was perhaps twenty-five hundred dollars. Scheer may have earned two hundred and fifty dollars, but his expenses had offset a big part of it. He had not expected to do better, he said, but he was frank in admitting that the results depressed him. He hastened to add that it was not the buyers' fault. He felt they had ordered about as many books as they could sell, with an exception or two— for instance, they had resisted "Weep No More, My Lady," Mickey Deans' book, written with Ann Pinchot, about Judy Garland, although Scheer expected it would sell quite well. Whenever such an order seemed too small to Scheer, he spoke up. He told most of the buyers that he thought they were underestimating the size of the Judy Garland cult. Everyone responded, as if they had been conferring on the point, that they had been too enthusiastic about two earlier Judy Garland books; they were afraid of getting stuck again with copies they would have to return. At Scheer's urging, the buyers would order a few additional copies of a title, or agree to try a copy or two of a book they were inclined to pass up, but Scheer seldom put pressure on them, and when he did, it was never great. When they thought they could not sell a book, Scheer accepted their verdict. (A salesman who oversells is, of course, confronted by every one of his errors, standing unsold on the bookstore's shelves, on his next

trip.) Often, the order was Scheer's suggestion. "I
don't know, George," the buyer would say. "How
many do you think I need?"

"Three or four," Scheer would answer.

In that case, the number ordered would most likely
be three.

But an order for three copies, which had sounded
pathetic to me early on Monday morning, sounded
pretty good by Tuesday night, because I had heard so
many "two"s and "one"s, and even more "none"s. A
five was heartwarming, a ten was excellent. There
were only a few orders for fifteen copies, and they
were mostly for backlist staples, like Tasha Tudor's
"First Prayers" for children, which had evidently been
selling splendidly in both its Catholic and its Protes-
tant editions.

I not only learned how hard it is to sell a hundred
copies of a book at the rate of three or four per store,
I saw how little time Scheer had to spend on any one
title. He was selling two hundred and six new books
—a hundred and fifty hardcovers and fifty-six paperbacks. (Among the latter, besides Irving Howe's book,
were "Last Reflections on a War," by the late Bernard
Fall, "What Black Politicians Are Saying," edited by
Nathan Wright, Jr., "Maple-Sugaring," by Myrtie and
Floyd Fellows, "Riddle Me This," by Frances Chrystie,
and "On Judaism," by Martin Buber.) It was not an
unusual number for him, or for any commission man,
nor was it more than many house salesmen handle.
Scheer had explained to me that a full-scale selling
session took all morning or all afternoon, and that
therefore he could take care of only two big accounts
a day. But I had not figured out that the time from ten
o'clock in the morning, which is when most book buy-

ers begin buying, to one o'clock is only a hundred and eighty minutes. And Scheer had a lot to do besides describe the merits of the books. In every store but one—Scheer told me it was the case in nine out of ten of the stores he calls on—he had to improvise a place to work. Most of the stores had desks, but they were loaded with correspondence, catalogues, invoices, and directories, which had to be pushed aside. The buyers had worked with scores of salesmen during the previous weeks, and yet they were as unprepared for Scheer's call as if it were an event without precedent.

Then there was a lot to talk about before the selling could begin. Scheer's mustache was new; he had had to grow it because he lost a bet with his son. It surprised everyone, and it had to be explained and evaluated. (The consensus was that it should stay.) The buyers wanted to know how Genevieve was, and whether his son, George, was liking his sophomore year at Brown University. Scheer, in turn, wanted to know about their families, and he passed along news of and regards from booksellers he had called on during the first part of his trip. And, invariably, the buyers wanted to tell Scheer that they felt that the publishers —all the publishers, not just the group Scheer was representing—were trying to drive them crazy. Some spoke angrily. Others sounded puzzled: "What in the world are they trying to *do* to us, George?" They all felt that inhuman forces were working against them, and all held the publishers responsible. Most of the illustrative stories had to do with books they had ordered that either had taken forever to arrive or had arrived all wrong or had arrived twice. There were complaints about errors in billing and errors in credits for returned books. The buyers were convinced that

once an error had occurred it was well-nigh uncorrect-
able. They asked Scheer to explain why publishers
need to keep revising their discount schedules. They
said that keeping track of ever-changing terms and
ever-changing credits for returned books was a full-
time occupation in itself. And, they asked, why
couldn't the publishers decide by the time the jacket
was printed what the retail price of a book was to be?
(Price changes that were announced after the booksellers had received the books meant that they had to
paste new prices, on gummed labels, on the jacket
flaps.) None of the buyers thought that Scheer could
do much about the sins of the publishers, except possibly those of the ones he was working for, and yet,
knowing that he would be in New York before very
long, talking to publishers, they spoke as if they felt he
might convey their messages. Whenever a specific
complaint was made about one of Scheer's publishers
—an order unfilled, a shipment billed twice, a letter
unanswered for weeks, or whatever—he got out a
pocket memo pad and wrote it down. "Inexcusable,"
Scheer would say. "It's all too much for the damned
computers, apparently, but I'll get on it right away."

There were frequent interruptions. Each buyer had
at least one assistant clerking in the store, but as the
authority on what was in stock or on order, each one,
except Kay Archer, at Maison Blanche, had to stop to
take phone calls. If two or three customers needed
attention at one time, the buyer would leave to help
wait on them; far from resenting this, Scheer helped
out, too, on several occasions. After he had gone
through a publisher's new books, he would spend
quite a bit of time on that firm's backlist. (A book goes
on the backlist the day it is published; some of the

books he talked about were only a few weeks old.) In the aggregate, Scheer's backlists contained two thousand five hundred and fifteen books, four-fifths of them hardcover. He did not need to say much about them. The buyers knew which books had been selling well—they just needed to be reminded of their titles. Besides the lists at the back of the publishers' catalogues, and on the backlist order forms, Scheer had a visual aid for two publishers' books which was a sort of miniature of his jacket-book—several hundred three-by-five color photographs of backlist jackets mounted in a small ring binder. He flipped them over quickly, with only occasional comments, and the buyers recognized those they wanted. In many cases, backlist orders were larger than new-book orders, and Scheer had trouble at times writing down the numbers as fast as the buyers spoke them. From time to time, an inventory question would arise. "It's been selling, but I think we've still got several copies left," a buyer would say. "You sold me too many on your last trip, George."

The moment Scheer entered a store, he began studying the shelves, and every time he lost the buyer's attention, even momentarily, he studied them further. What was on display was approximately what was in stock, because, except for Maison Blanche, no one had much storage space. Scheer was often able to say authoritatively, "You're down to two. I just counted them. I think you can use another five." If he did not know how many copies were on hand, he got up, walked to the appropriate section, and looked. That sometimes led to some shelf-straightening, and a few additional seconds' elapsed time. (Scheer hates to see the copies of one title scattered; it is axiomatic among booksellers that the more copies you have of a title the faster it moves.)

What with all the diversions and distractions, I estimated that Scheer spent only half his time selling his new titles. Many of them were disposed of in seconds. He would turn a page of the jacket-book and read a title, and before he could finish his handle the buyer would reject the book: "I think I'd better skip that one, George," or "Let's go on," or, sometimes, just plain "No." A fast negative was often accompanied by an apology: "I'm sure it's a good book, George, but there simply isn't any interest around here in art criticism." Most of the books called for some consideration. When a buyer knew on sight that she wanted to order some copies of a particular book but did not know how many, it took her a while to make up her mind. Scheer often suggested a number, but he never seemed to hurry the decision. He sounded willing to talk indefinitely about any title. I knew that if a buyer wanted to hear more, Scheer was prepared to say more, because he had at least sampled all the new books—except for a few he had not been able to get, even in galleys. He had read twenty or thirty with care, including some he had not liked at all. Scheer never says he likes a book he doesn't like; in that case, he simply doesn't bring up the fact that he has read it. If he is cornered, he tells the truth, and reminds the buyer, "But my personal reaction has no more to do with whether it will sell than yours will have." The buyers listened to Scheer, between interruptions, with close attention; they were hungry for information, and intent on visualizing the finished books from the evidence of the jackets. They often did reach out, as Scheer had anticipated, to feel the jackets and swing them on their hinges. (It would

be much easier but less effective, Scheer feels, to
mount the jackets in transparent plastic envelopes.)
Although none of the buyers said so, I felt that, for all
their seriousness, they were slightly disappointed.
They looked forward to a number of his books, but
they were hoping for something great that was sure to
sell extremely well, and on this trip they did not find
it.

Allowing for everything, Scheer was able to devote
about ninety out of each hundred and eighty minutes
to pure new-book selling—a little more than twenty-
six seconds, on the average, for each of his two hundred and six new titles. There were a number of five-
second or ten-second books, briefly described and
quickly rejected. Still, when Scheer did have his full
say he spent about a minute on a book. I could not
help thinking that that was all he would have for another "Moby Dick."

Tuesday night, on schedule, we were driving
through a drizzle on Interstate 10, headed for Baton
Rouge. Scheer said, "Now you understand why at one
sales conference after another my voice is raised with
my annoying question: 'Well and good, but what is the
*handle?* What can I tell the buyers?' I often think how
shocked authors would be if they listened to the salesmen selling their books. They've worked for a year on
their book—two years, three years, maybe longer. And
there it is. A word or two and the decision is made. I
am not selling faster than other salesmen; on the contrary, I am kidded about having too much to say. I
don't think many authors could stand it."

And yet, Scheer said, he feels that the selling-buying
process is less haphazard than an author might think.

"Naturally, I seldom feel that I have done justice to the nuances of any real work of art," he said. "But I can usually look over my tally sheets at the end of a trip and see that I've achieved a reasonably good spread for it—let's say that two-thirds of my accounts have ordered at least a copy or two. The book has a chance, assuming that all the other salesmen have done about equally well. If two booksellers out of three have it on publication day, at least it is alive. Books *have* survived a wretched advance sale; that is, you can collect anecdotes, if you care to, about slow starters, ignored for a long time, that have gone on to good sales, even great sales. It happens, but it is very rare. I can almost never expect a good reorder on a second trip if I haven't had a good order on my first—not unless something truly extraordinary has happened in the meantime: a National Book Award, a Pulitzer, or the Nobel Prize. Most good reorders represent the experience of the particular bookseller. A kind of momentum has developed. Say she took five initially. They disappeared fast, and she has no doubt that the store can sell five more, or even ten, because her customers are talking to each other about the book. A buyer for a small bookstore is in very close touch with that reality—although there are enough surprises every season to make life interesting. Don't be deceived by my buyers' politeness. They know almost instantly how many copies they can sell, and I doubt whether their estimates would improve much if they took ten times as long to buy. Fiction is harder to predict than nonfiction. If I am selling for a house that runs heavily to fiction, I know, and my accounts know, that the returns on that list are going to be high. Of course, there's an exception to every generalization about bookselling;

ordinarily, it is hard to raise high expectations for nonfiction, whereas the mere mention of a famous novelist's name is exciting. But novels stall. The salesmen get out a good advance of thirty thousand, everything looks fine, and they follow up with ten thousand more. Unaccountably, the customers stop buying at twenty-eight thousand, and twelve thousand copies are headed right back to the publisher.

"Bookstore buyers are cautious because returns are a nightmare. The booksellers don't buy on consignment, as many people think. It is a real sale. They get credit for returns, but full credit is not easy to come by. The books must be in good condition, must be properly packed, and must be returned within a specified time. If the bookstore has mislaid the original invoice, some publishers assume that the store got a bigger discount than it really did. Even under the best circumstances, the bookstore loses on returns, because it has to pay the return shipping costs, but a more substantial loss is all the paperwork and time involved. I hate to see the returns on the books I've sold get as high as fifteen per cent, although I understand that the national average for all publishers is nearly twenty per cent. Like all salesmen, I'm under constant pressure on this. If my returns are low, my publishers suspect me of underselling. If I sell too hard and returns are high, my accounts turn me off. It's a tightrope. Not every bookstore buyer is a genius, you understand. Some buyers just plain annoy me. My bête noire is the buyer who says, 'Oh, I see you have a new book about Taiwan. Have you seen Harper's new book about Indo-China?,' and proceeds to tell me all about Harper's new book. Still, my three hundred buyers buy wisely, in the aggregate. When I run into resistance on a title, I call Roger, and I find, almost invariably, that he is running into resistance, too. And I'm almost willing to bet that the East has been bad, the West has been bad, and the Middle West has been bad, too. The author, the publisher, and the salesmen have all been dreaming pipe dreams, and the book-store buyers, in their collective wisdom, have brought us back to earth.''

Business improved as Scheer and I travelled west from New Orleans. Early Wednesday morning, he got an excellent order at Claitor's, a huge bookstore on the southern outskirts of Baton Rouge, in a building that looks like a factory. Actually, it is an adjunct of a publishing operation, where a man named Robert Claitor produces regional, technical, and legal books. It has half a dozen clerks, trimly dressed stockroom girls, and a vast selling area with bookshelves rising all around to a double-height ceiling. (The shelves that cannot be reached except by ladder are used for stor-age; there is also a big stockroom at the back of the store.) Sometimes Mrs. Claitor does the buying but she was away, and an assistant, Cecile Bourgeois, was taking her place. She was tidy and precise, and al-though she sometimes hesitated over a title, she knew exactly what Claitor's wanted. Almost every time Scheer turned to the next page in his jacket-book, Miss Bourgeois rolled her eyes heavenward, as if to say, "My goodness, what will they think of next?" She said hardly a word except "I'll take ten," or whatever the number was; she ordered some copies of almost every new title; and there was a sprinkling of twenty-fives among the numbers. There seemed to be an added spring to Scheer's step as we walked back to his car.

We went on to Melvin Shortess's small store, Shortess Paper Books—a misnomer, for perhaps a quarter
of the stock was hardcover—in one of the blocks bor-
dering Louisiana State University. Melvin and his wife,
Helen, are among Scheer's oldest friends; he had
taken them to dinner, after drinks at their home, a
handsome house in the suburbs, the night before.
Until a few years ago, the Shortesses ran a much larger
bookstore downtown, in the main business district of
Baton Rouge. They regard Shortess Paper Books,
about a mile from where they live, and hardly more
than twenty feet wide and thirty feet deep, as semi-
retirement; they can run the whole business by themselves, working six days a week. Selling at Shortess
Paper Books took Scheer no more than an hour.
Shortess wanted quite a few titles—his customers are
mostly university students, and the Schocken backlist,
strong on education, Kafka, religion, and philosophy,
had a good deal of what he needed—but because his
tiny store has no stockroom he bought in small quantities.

By midafternoon, we were on the road to Beaumont, Texas, having stopped, just to say hello, at the
offices of the L.S.U. Press. The press had several trade
books on its list besides Havard's "The Changing Politics of the South"—including a biography of Ellen
Glasgow by E. Stanly Godbold, Jr., and "Hugo Black:
The Alabama Years," by Virginia Van der Veer Hamil-
ton—and Scheer was able to report that sales had
been going reasonably well.

The skies broke open as we entered Beaumont.
Scheer had to stop driving for a few minutes; the cas-
cade of water was too much for the windshield wipers.
Then it let up slightly, and we turned in at the next

motel we came to, a Ramada Inn, where he had not made a reservation. I was surprised, but Scheer explained that he makes reservations at only a few motels on his route, in order to have some mail addresses. "If I made reservations all the way, I'd just have to change them every time I got off schedule, and that would take hours. If I hit a storm like this one, I want to be able to stop. It's tourists who make reservations, because they're afraid of being shut out completely. The motels that cater primarily to travelling salesmen are seldom sold out. When one is, I know another that isn't. On weekends, of course, they're practically empty. Every salesman who can possibly make it has gone streaking for home."

Scheer had to write several letters, fill in the headings on the order forms—the names and addresses of the stores, the dates, the names of the buyers, and the order numbers—and make some long-distance calls. He was putting in two hours of office work a night, usually between ten and midnight, and we were regularly breakfasting at seven-thirty. Yet, as far as I could tell, Scheer was thriving on his seventeen- or eighteen-hour days. "It's true," he said. "I am exhilarated by it. I suppose it does not really seem like work to me. It takes a lot of energy, but I don't notice that unless I get sick on a trip. I have to laugh, though, when people ask, 'What is there to do at night?' As you have seen, I work at night, when I am not having dinner with friends. As I recall, I've been to the movies on the road twice in the past ten years."

Scheer had only two calls to make in Beaumont the next day, Thursday. He called on Reta Piland, head librarian of the Jefferson County Library—a most unusual account. Libraries seldom buy from trade-

book salesmen; rather, they rely on institutional jobbers or specialized school, university, and institutional
salesmen. Mrs. Piland ordered a lot of titles, and, because she was buying for a main library and three
branch libraries, in most cases she thought of four
copies almost as one.

At the Key Book Shop, our other planned stop in
Beaumont, Scheer was told that Tom Clemmons, the
owner, was out to lunch. He took the news philosoph-
ically. It is a small store, heavily slanted toward best-
sellers and popular nonfiction, and Scheer introduced
himself to the salesgirl (the first time on our trip that
he had had to introduce himself), chatted with her
about what he discovered was her home town—Boston—and, while he talked, went through a set of his
catalogues, marking a title here and a title there, perhaps twenty-five or thirty in all. He handed the marked
catalogues to the girl. "Give Tom my best, and tell him
I'm sorry to miss seeing him," he said. "I'd wait, but
I've got to move on to Houston. And Tom needn't
worry. I've marked everything he'll want to consider."
With that, we were gone. The call had taken not more
than twenty minutes.

As we drove, Scheer told me that ordinarily he
counts marking the catalogues, the way he had just
done, as a poor substitute for selling but that this case
was not so bad. "Tom Clemmons really does not want
to hear what I have to say about the books," he explained. "He just wants to know which books will be
advertised or listed in *Book Chat.*" Then Scheer realized he had to explain that *Book Chat* is a bi-monthly
publication, produced in Chicago, that describes
eighty or ninety new books in its editorial columns.
Local bookstores' names are imprinted on it, and the

stores distribute it to their customers; the back cover includes two prepaid tear-out postcards addressed to a particular store, to be used as order forms. "*Book Chat* puts out a huge Christmas issue, and there are several Christmas-gift catalogues of the same sort, imprinted the same way," Scheer said. "They are influential. All my accounts want to know what is going to be in *Book Chat* and the Christmas catalogues. It's something I note in the jacket-book whenever I have the information. How do customers hear about the existence of a new book? It is hard to accept the fact that not everyone reads the *Times Book Review* every week, but we have to face it. People expect their bookseller to tell them what has been published. The bookstore·has a news-bearing function. And *Book Chat* is one of the ways it fulfills it."

By late afternoon, we were in Houston, and Scheer's spirits were effervescent. "Now we're in a real book town," he said. "Houston is a city where I drive seventy-five miles a day inside the city limits and don't ever mind it. No matter how badly a trip may have been going, Houston revives me." Scheer has watched Houston grow, since 1946, from a city he could cover in two days into one that occupies him for at least seven, and sometimes ten. (His second-longest stop, of four or five days, is in Dallas.) He would not be in the least surprised, he said, if within less than a decade Houston rose to fourth place in the ranking of book-buying cities. There was a stack of mail, including a tape cassette from Hawthorn, waiting for Scheer at the Travelodge Motel; Hawthorn, as an experiment, was equipping its salesmen with cassette recorders to facilitate two-way communication with the sales manager.

Before he read his letters or listened to the cassette, Scheer was on the telephone talking to Ted Brown, another good friend. At the time, Brown owned two bookstores in Houston: Brown Book Shop, in the heart of the old downtown business district, the best-known bookstore in the Southwest, and Brown's Post Oak, in the Post Oak shopping complex, part of one of the city's several satellite downtowns. Houston had a hundred and fifty suburban shopping centers at last count, but the Post Oak-Westheimer complex, a glittering expanse of white buildings and gray parking lots just off the vast oval freeway system, is the eye-opener. In addition to Brown's Post Oak, the area includes such attractions as Sakowitz, Neiman-Marcus, and Joske's—all department stores—and the Galleria, which is an enclosed, air-conditioned shopping mall on three levels, with around a hundred shops, an ice-skating rink, an art gallery, and two movie theatres.

Brown told Scheer he was getting ready to close the downtown store for the day but said there was time for us to get there if we hurried, so we hurried. A tall, dapper man with a flamboyant mustache, given to boldly striped shirts, Brown seems to qualify well for Scheer's encomium "a real bookman." He not only loves books but manages his stores with attention to every detail. He presides over the downtown store, like a captain on the bridge of a ship, from a square combination counter and office just inside the plate-glass doors. The store is a big, no-nonsense place with a large stock—rows of books on racks and shelves, many with just their spines visible. It looks cluttered, but Brown, who has thirteen saleswomen and salesmen working for him, knows exactly where every book is. The downtown store is patronized predominantly by men, and stocks a lot of books on business, economics, science, art, and history. (It carries, for instance, all of Samuel Eliot Morison's fifteen-volume "History of United States Naval Operations in World War II.") Brown's Post Oak is more for women, and tidiness is its hallmark; the books are well displayed, and the emphasis is on fiction, cookbooks, and the household arts. Brown has a reputation for being tough on book salesmen. He is uncommonly knowledgeable about books, and art books are a specialty of his. (A salesman once showed him advance proofs of a splendid collection of Picasso's work in which one abstraction was reproduced upside down; Brown recognized the error instantly and was the first to report it to the publisher.) He barks at salesmen who assume that hyperbole will impress him. Since Scheer knows Brown well, he not only refrains from hyperbole but when Brown barks he barks right back.

Brown told us that his wife, Sylvia, who runs the Post Oak store, was there and would not be leaving for a little while, so we drove out to say hello to her—about six miles through a succession of residential districts with names like River Oaks, Tall Timbers, and Afton Oaks. Scheer chatted with Sylvia Brown for a few minutes, and then we drove to another bookstore, named Cobler's Book Store, at Post Oak for a chat with its buyer, Bill Caskey. (Two other places also sell books in the Post Oak-Westheimer area: the book department of Joske's, and the Sam Houston Book Shop, in the Galleria.)

Scheer started selling in earnest the following day. That was Friday, and it was his ambition to finish Houston by the following Thursday, in time to drive the two hundred miles to San Antonio, his next stop, that evening; he could make it if his appointments dropped into place perfectly. Counting the Post Oak-Westheimer area stores, Scheer had thirteen buyers, buying for twenty bookstores, on his list; among his first calls were those on Bill Streich, of Bookland; Brian Sumrall, of Books Incorporated; Jean Ball, of Jean's Book Shoppe; and Jessie Allen, of Allen-Maxwell Books. He hoped if possible, to enlarge the list. He knew of a couple of new stores he had never called on, and if time permitted he wanted at least to scout them out and see whether they were worth adding to his future trips. Scheer's pace through New Orleans, Baton Rouge, and Beaumont had awed me. It was clear that in Houston he intended to step it up.

At our seven-thirty breakfast on Friday in the motel's dining room, Scheer told me, over enormous glasses of Texas orange juice, that he had been up and working for a couple of hours, answering letters and listening to the Hawthorn cassette. "They gave me a few compliments, but mostly they gave me hell," he said of the message on the cassette. "The sales manager thinks I am not doing well enough with Emily Gardiner Neal's book, 'The Healing Power of Christ' —not as well as his other salesmen, that is. I'm sure he suspects me of skipping some religious bookstores, but I think the whole thing is a misunderstanding. I'm nearly a month behind the rest of the Hawthorn men, and I think—I *hope*—he is comparing my very early figures with their much more complete results. Anyhow, I checked my figures on the Neal up through Beaumont, and they look all right. I know for sure that I have not been skipping the religious bookstores. First chance I get, I'll dictate an up-to-date report, and maybe the sales manager will feel better."

Scheer looked rather distressed, and I asked whether he resented being scolded, especially by a tape recording. His frown immediately changed to a broad smile. "It's quite the other way around," he said. "Naturally, I don't want to be scolded at all, but I could be missing a trick without realizing it. He also asked me what handle I am using on 'Home Landscaping You Can Design Yourself,' so he can pass the word on to the other men. Apparently, my figures on that one are excellent. I admire the way Hawthorn is keeping on top of the sales picture. That's what it should be doing, and it's doing it well."

In the course of the week, Scheer managed to fit in all his accounts. He never stopped if it was at all possible to keep going; Sunday he devoted to writing up orders, writing letters, answering Hawthorn's tape, taking his mail to the main post office, and dining at the Ted Browns'. He was pleased by the orders he got, especially the one from Brown. Scheer guessed that, in all, the orders were about ten per cent bigger, in dollars, than those a year earlier; nearly all the buyers said that their sales were up by about that percentage since then. Scheer also made time before, after, and between his main appointments for quite a little scouting. He looked in on a camping-equipment store on Westbury Square, thinking that it might be interested in stocking a few copies of a Schocken book called "Bushcraft: A Serious Guide to Survival and Camping," by Richard Graves. But the official opening of the shop was a few days off, and a busy young man who was assembling a bright-orange portable tent said he believed that there was a plan to have a shelf of camping books for sale but he wasn't sure. Scheer said he would try to stop by on his next trip. He investigated a wholesaler called Houston Health Food Distributors; two of his new books were "Cooking Creatively with Natural Foods," by Sam and Edith Brown, and "Putting Food By," by Ruth Hertzberg, Beatrice Vaughan, and Janet Greene, and Scheer sold the firm some of these books. If Scheer had an appointment for two o'clock and we had finished lunch by one o'clock, he would remember some place he could go for a quick visit. We stopped at Stelzig Saddlery Company, which sells saddles, boots, guns, and Western hats and clothes. Scheer loves the store, and has stopped there many times before. As a result, it has a small shelf of how-to books about riding and the training of horses. Scheer was worried because his titles did not seem to have been selling well. It was evident to me that Leo Stelzig, Jr., who runs the Saddlery, was not worried, in view of the number of customers who were buying two-hundred-and-seventy-five-dollar boots. Nevertheless, Scheer spent more than an hour in the store. He rearranged the books on the shelf, extracted extra copies of a few titles that needed to be returned, and told Stelzig he had a few new books that belonged in the inventory. Stelzig was happy to go along with whatever Scheer suggested. Then Scheer helped Stelzig carry the returns to the Saddlery shipping room and pack them in cardboard cartons. For lack of other packing-case filler—at least, there was none right at hand—Stelzig filled in the crevices with scraps of high-grade woolly sheepskin, of the kind used to line Stelzig saddles. I wondered what the publishers' warehousemen would think when they opened the cartons. "Of course, spending all that time did not make sense," Scheer said as we drove out of the Saddlery parking lot. "Even if Stelzig's book department quadrupled in size—which, obviously, it is not likely to do—I should not have stayed so long. But if I had to think I couldn't afford a little foolishness, I'd prefer to give up the whole thing. I like talking to Leo Stelzig, and his store delights me. On top of that—my fatal weakness, I suppose—the thought that I may be able to sell three more copies of one of my books, say, 'The Cowboy Trade,' by Glen Rounds, is catnip to the old cat."

On Wednesday, I had to leave Scheer, in order to keep an appointment in New York. By Tuesday night, he was so confident of finishing Houston on time that he had decided to drive down to the Manned Space-craft Center, thirty-two miles southeast of town, to see friends who had no connection at all with books—former colleagues of Julian Scheer, his younger brother, who had spent nine years as the assistant administrator for public affairs of NASA. Scheer and I had dinner at a Steak & Ale restaurant. "I do wish you could see San Antonio," Scheer said. "It doesn't have Houston's razzle-dazzle—this marvelous mixture of sophistication with the frontier conviction that everything is possible—but San Antonio, I suppose, is even more colorful, in an entirely different way. And it's interesting from a book point of view. I have two big quality-paperback accounts there—retailers with chains of paperback stores—a department store, three or four nice personal bookshops, and two truly fine old-time bookstores."

Scheer remarked that under the expansive Houston skies it was hard to realize that some of the handsome, well-arranged, busy bookstores we had been visiting were operating on the thinnest of economic margins. "They are no different from bookstores everywhere else," he said. "They don't know for sure whether they will wind up in the red or the black for the year until the Christmas rush is over. Christmas saves them, ordinarily. They may do a third of their annual business, or more, in November and December. There have never been as many bookstores in Houston as there are now, but there have been too many failures along the way.

"When any small business is trimmed close," Scheer said, "and every nickel and dime counts, there is no room for a mistake. A busy bookstore may gross a hundred thousand a year. That means it has to have space for a thirty- or thirty-five-thousand-dollar inventory—say, eight to ten thousand books. A bookstore selling a half-million dollars' worth of books is a landmark, known all over the state. Ted Brown won't tell what his gross is—it's even bigger than that—and, at least within the trade, Brown is famous all over the country. But say you are selling that hundred thousand dollars' worth of books, taking advantage of every strategy and getting maximum discounts. You are paying only some sixty-two to sixty-four thousand dollars for your books, including postage, so ostensibly you have a thirty-six-to-thirty-eight-thousand-dollar profit. But you have to have at least one clerk. You also need a high-school boy who can come in during the late afternoons to help you move the newly arrived book cartons and open them. There's the rent, upkeep, and electricity—and in Houston, at least, you must be air-conditioned. If you buy wisely, your shipping charges on returns will not be much more than a few hundred dollars for the year. And so, if your accountant does not charge too much, and if you refrain from spending too heavily on local advertising, if your insurance isn't too expensive, and if pilferage doesn't run too high, and if almost all of your charge-account customers pay their bills, then it is possible—just possible—that you may have fifteen or sixteen thousand dollars left before taxes. Of course, you have not taken any salary for yourself. But that is the ideal. The real bookseller makes mistakes, all down the line. An accident of any kind—a couple of small robberies, say—can break his back. He does not have the financial strength to survive a serious reversal of any kind. And so you find hundreds of towns big enough to support a bookstore that don't have any. When one went broke, nobody was foolish enough to start another. When a bookstore closes, the book business it was generating often seems to evaporate—it's like the circulation of a newspaper that folds. Where does that business go? Some of it may go miles and miles away —the town's book addicts may drive ninety miles, on Saturday afternoons, to pick up an armful of books at some place like Ted Brown's. Some of it goes to the Book-of-the-Month Club, or another mail-order source. Most of it, I'm convinced, just stops. People quit reading books and turn on television, because they do not have a bookseller who can inspire them to read by telling them what there is to read and by making books seem valuable and exciting and fashionable.

"It takes both talent and industry to operate a successful bookshop. There are people, fortunately, who have enough of both. And an adroit bookseller can make a good living for a lifetime, in a joyous occupation. I do think publishers need to help bookstores in every possible way. It's crucial. Nobody else does what the dedicated bookseller does. Trade publishing must have outlets for good trade books, and to have them it has to give those outlets support.

"For my own part, as a liaison between my publishers and my bookstores, I like to think I'm helping to keep the bookstores alive and healthy—a contribution, in a small way, to the survival of American letters."

# CHAPTER 6

# A Better Sound

## CYRIL M. HARRIS

DECEMBER, 1974: On Tuesday the third, Amyas Ames, the retired investment banker who is chairman of the board of directors of the Lincoln Center for the Performing Arts, telephoned Professor Cyril M. Harris, of Columbia University. Harris teaches courses in acoustics at Columbia's School of Engineering and its School of Architecture, and, every second year, a course on noise pollution at its Law School. Primarily a scientist, he has done research in acoustics for thirty-five years and taught it for twenty-five. As a sideline, he also does acoustical consulting. Ever since 1940, when he was still a graduate student, working for his doctoral degree in physics at the Massachusetts Institute of Technology, Harris has advised clients on many kinds of problems involving noise, sound, and vibration. Over the years, auditorium acoustics, which had always been his first love, gradually became his consulting specialty. In all, he has designed or helped design more than a hundred auditoriums. Some are lecture halls, meeting halls, or boardrooms, but most are for the performing arts— theatres, opera houses, and concert halls. The acoustics of some are good, and some are superlatively good, but none are bad—a record that is not even approached, much less matched, by that of any other acoustical consultant in the world.

When Ames told Harris he wanted to speak to him about the acoustics of Avery Fisher Hall, Harris's heart sank. Harris ordinarily loves to discuss acoustics, but he did not want to talk about Avery Fisher Hall, Lincoln Center's handsome twelve-year-old concert hall, built as a permanent home for the New York Philharmonic. Even after a quarter century of lecturing on acoustics an average of six hours a week during the academic year, Harris talks to his students about the production, transmission, and effects of sound with the delight of a discoverer, as if he had come upon the ideas only moments earlier; but for twelve years he had scrupulously refrained from commenting on the acoustics of Avery Fisher Hall—or Philharmonic Hall, as it was called until 1973, when it was renamed for a philanthropist who became its chief benefactor. Harris had not wanted to criticize the work of a rival expert, Leo L. Beranek, of the consulting firm Bolt Beranek & Newman, of Cambridge, Massachusetts, who had been the chief acoustical consultant to Harris's friend Max Abramovitz, the architect of the building; nor had Harris wanted to disparage the efforts of the half-dozen acousticians who had attempted to improve the sound of the auditorium during the summers of 1963, 1964, 1965, 1969, and 1972, and whose efforts, all of them unsuccessful, had cost

somewhat more than two million dollars. There was
another consideration. Though talking to Ames was
entirely different from discussing Avery Fisher Hall in
public, or for quotation, and would thus not violate
Harris's standards of professional courtesy, he suspected that Ames might suggest that he, Harris, *do*
something about the hall, and Harris did not think that
anything could be done. Experience had taught him
that it is extremely difficult for an acoustical consultant
to tell a prospective client, "I'd like to help, but there
is no solution." Harris had been compelled to say that
quite a few times—especially after he had helped re-
model an old movie palace into Powell Symphony
Hall, for the St. Louis Symphony Orchestra, in 1968.
The results had been glorious in every way, but particularly glorious acoustically, and Harris had been beset
ever since by inquiries from prominent citizens in
other cities with old movie houses, who wanted Harris
to do something similar for their symphony orchestras. Harris loves the notion of preserving old buildings, and he had examined a few candidates for remodelling, but he had not found another semi-antique
odeon that he felt could be made over to satisfy acoustical dreams. Also in his memory were several new
halls, built in the fifties, the sixties, or the early seventies, at costs of millions of dollars, that had turned out
to be acoustic lemons. Harris had been asked four or
five times, either by old friends or by architects he did
not know but whose work he admired, to take a look
at such problem halls and explain how they could be
fixed. He had gone and looked—some acoustical
faults *can* be repaired—but in every case he had been
compelled to say that the acoustics were so bad that no
amount of renovation would help. And every time

Harris had said, "No, it won't do. Don't try it," he had
hurt someone's feelings. Harris, a sensitive and polite
man, had found these occasions painful. He did not
want to risk going through a similar unhappy scene
with Ames if he could avoid it.

Ames heard the reluctance in Harris's voice, but had
no idea why it was there. Harris heard himself, too,
and realized that it would be preposterous to refuse
even to talk to Amyas Ames. "Well, sure," he said.
"How about meeting me at my apartment tomorrow
morning after breakfast for a cup of coffee?"

The next morning, December 4th, Ames arrived at
Harris's apartment, on the East Side in the upper Seventies, at eight-thirty. Harris had, as usual, been awake
since six o'clock, and had finished breakfast and the
*Times* shortly after seven. He had been working at his
desk for nearly an hour and a half before he opened
the door to Ames and led him into the living room,
overlooking Central Park. It is decorated in white and
off-white, and has a very thick, sound-absorbing wall-
to-wall carpet. Coffee and pastries had been set out on
a low table in front of a sofa. Harris wished he could
explain how he felt about Avery Fisher Hall right
away, before the conversation started, but he re-
strained himself.

Ames is an impressive figure, tall and dignified, with
the self-confidence of an aristocrat, which in American
terms he is. He was at that time sixty-eight years old.
He speaks with what was once called a "Harvard accent," which had nothing to do with his having attended Harvard (class of 1928) and the Harvard Business School (class of 1930) and everything to do with
his having been born and brought up in Massachusetts, where the Ames family has lived since long be-

fore the Revolutionary War. The Ames Shovel & Tool Company, founded by Captain John Ames, of the Continental Army, turned out to be extremely profitable around the middle of the nineteenth century, to the considerable comfort of the Captain's descendants. Oakes Ames, Amyas Ames's father, was a distinguished Harvard professor of botany, a supervisor of the Arnold Arboretum, and a world authority on orchids. Ames is not only the head of Lincoln Center but also chairman of the board of the Philharmonic Symphony Society of New York, which was organized in 1842 and has kept the orchestra playing, through good times and bad, ever since. He works hard at both his jobs, keeping regular office hours and allowing himself only a few weeks' vacation in the summer, but he draws no salary; he regards his contribution of time and energy as his civic duty.

Harris listened while Ames explained that Lincoln Center had decided to "take hold" of the hall's acoustic problems, all previous frustrations, disappointments, and expenditures notwithstanding. It was a matter of necessity, said Ames—in fact, of several necessities. The orchestra members could not hear each other, and therefore could not be expected to play at their best. Audiences were hearing only part of what the orchestra was playing. In musical circles, the hall's acoustics were criticized on every hand, and the criticism was mounting. Beyond this, an economic disaster was in the making. Lincoln Center rents the hall whenever its prime tenant, the Philharmonic, isn't using it; rentals had fallen off, and the situation was likely to get worse, as visiting orchestras, chamber groups, and soloists decided they might sound better elsewhere—in Carnegie Hall, in the Hunter College

Assembly Hall, or even in the far smaller Kaufmann
Concert Hall, in the Ninety-second Street Y. Lincoln
Center had decided that, whatever was to be done,
there should be a fresh start, with a new architect and
a new acoustician; it wanted to write a brand-new
chapter with a brand-new team. Harris could hardly
keep from interrupting. However, Ames continued,
Lincoln Center did not know what could be done. The
board needed the advice— "the counsel"—of an un-
doubted authority, who would define the problem and
the possibilities. And, Ames said, the board realized
that there was just one such man—by good luck, a New
Yorker—and he was Cyril Harris.

At that point, Harris could contain himself no
longer, and, in terms as strong as he could make them,
he told Ames that he wanted nothing to do with Avery
Fisher Hall—absolutely *nothing,* ever. Under any circumstances. Ames was astonished. He had seldom
heard such a vehement "No." Then Ames got angry.
"Now, just a minute," he said. "You really ought to
think who you are saying no to. It is not to me. You
are saying no to all the people in this city who love
music. What are they going to do? You are saying no
to the listeners, you are saying no to the performing
artists. The Philharmonic is in trouble, and you are
saying no to it. You are saying that New York's great
orchestra can't have your attention. You can't *do* that!
You are saying no to the City of New York. Can we
pretend to be a great musical center and not have a
great place to hear music? Music is of the deepest
consequence to this city. And you are saying, 'I won't
have anything to do with my city'!"

Harris was moved and impressed. It struck him that
Ames was right. Although Harris was born in Detroit

and grew up in Hollywood, he loves New York City, except for its unnecessary noises; he felt that indeed he did have an obligation, as a citizen of New York, to help it if he could. Having just released all his negative feelings, he now felt sufficiently relaxed to offer some advice. "What I *could* do," he said, "is to take a look at the architectural drawings."

Three other men besides Ames were actively engaged in taking hold of the acoustic problems of Avery Fisher Hall. They were John W. Mazzola, a forty-six-year-old lawyer, formerly with the firm of Milbank, Tweed, Hadley & McCloy, who had become managing director of Lincoln Center, Inc., in 1968; Carlos Moseley, sixty years old, the concert pianist who had been managing director of the Philharmonic throughout the sixties, and its president since 1970; and Avery Fisher, sixty-eight, who was the retired chief executive of the Fisher Radio Corporation, an enterprise he had founded in the late nineteen thirties, and who, in September, 1973, had given Lincoln Center ten million dollars for "maintaining, operating, and improving" the concert hall. Ames had organized this committee of four after the first series of informal Rug Concerts, in the summer of 1973, for which the seats on the main floor of the hall had been removed, a carpet laid down, and squares of foam rubber scattered about, so that concertgoers could sprawl on the floor instead of sitting decorously in rows of seats. The orchestra, instead of playing in its usual position onstage, had also come down onto the floor—but with its chairs and music stands—and occupied the space normally taken by the first several rows of seats. Everybody had enjoyed these performances, and quite a few people, including some critics, had said that they felt the acoustics were improved by the odd arrangement. The response to the Rug Concerts awakened hopes that had been dormant since the disappointing results of the last remodelling. Perhaps a solution would be to move the orchestra forward on a permanent basis, and to create a concert hall in the semiround—something that had not been previously contemplated. (It did not seem practical, however, to ask the Philharmonic's regular subscribers to lounge on the floor.) Ames, Mazzola, Moseley, and Fisher had been investigating that idea for more than a year, consulting with Dr. M. R. Schroeder, of the Bell Telephone Laboratories, and several other experts, including Stephen F. Temmer, of the Gotham Audio Corporation. Designs had been drawn and a fascinating scale model built. The trouble was that moving the orchestra forward permanently would cost quite a lot, and there was still doubt about how much good it would do acoustically. One of the reasons for talking with Harris was to find out what he thought of the repositioning scheme.

As soon as Ames had Harris's mild concession, Ames hurried across Central Park to the Lincoln Center offices, which are not at Lincoln Center but in the American Bible Society Building, on Broadway at Sixty-first Street. Mazzola was at his desk in his office, which is next to Ames's office. "I've got the break," Ames said. "Harris will look at the plans. For goodness' sakes, let's get them to him fast. Use the pony express if you have to." ("The pony express," in Lincoln Center office parlance, means that if a messenger is not immediately available a member of the staff makes the delivery.) Before noon, the plans were at Harris's apartment.

From time to time during the next several days, Harris studied the Avery Fisher Hall blueprints. Though he had never examined them before, he started out with considerable knowledge of the auditorium's acoustical faults. Harris and his wife, Ann, who is a senior editor at the publishing house of Harper & Row, are devoted concertgoers; they had attended scores of concerts in the hall since its inauguration, in late September of 1962, when they went to the introductory performances during the gala opening week (Harris had saved his blue-and-gold souvenir program). After each of the attempts to fix up the sound, Harris had noted that more work needed to be done. Like all New York music lovers, Harris had read what the critics had written. He had also followed the technical literature on the hall in various publications, including *The Journal of the Acoustical Society of America,* which had printed "Acoustics of Philharmonic Hall, New York, During its First Season," by Leo L. Beranek, F. R. Johnson, Theodore J. Schultz, and B. G. Watters, all of Bolt Beranek & Newman, in 1964; and "Acoustical Measurements in Philharmonic Hall (New York)," by M. R. Schroeder, B. S. Atal, G. M. Sessler, and J. E. West, all of the Bell Telephone Laboratories, in 1966. (Harris had been president of the Acoustical Society in 1964 and 1965, and an associate editor of the *Journal* from 1959 to 1970.)

The evidence of his ears had told Harris what was wrong with the sound in Avery Fisher Hall. Each of the modifications had slightly improved matters, but the acoustical faults remained much the same as they had been originally. For one thing, the orchestra sounded dry and lifeless. In a great hall, a member of the audience feels immersed in sound, but in Avery Fisher he felt that the music was coming directly to him from the stage; he had no sense of being in a room filled with music—he did not feel the sound's vibration with his feet, as he would in a great concert hall. For another thing, he heard far too little bass compared to treble; no matter how loud they played, the cellos and the double basses were too weak. Then, in some unhappy seat locations there were echoes, so that a single note sounded like two notes. And the orchestra was worse off than the audience; onstage, the musicians could not hear what they or their neighbors were playing. Ames, Mazzola, Moseley, and Fisher knew all this as well as Harris did. Their question was, what could be done about it?

Harris had spread the plans out on a desk. Each page was almost as big as the desk top, and there were twenty or twenty-five pages of drawings. He stood up to read them, leaning over the desk, making an occasional mark with a red pencil. From time to time, he jotted down a note on a separate pad of paper, but he did not make any mathematical calculations or employ any of the hundreds of acoustic equations and formulas that he keeps in his head. Harris reads architectural plans as easily as a conductor reads orchestral scores; to his practiced eyes the acoustical merits and demerits of a design simply leap off the page. He is a compact, slight man of average height, and is possessed of superabundant energy. It is hard for him to sit still, and he abhors unfilled time. He has dark hair, worn short, and although that December, when he was fifty-seven, it was becoming a trifle thin, he looked at least ten years younger than he was. He wore—as he still wears—glasses with dark frames. Harris's expression as he pored over the blueprints was one of rueful displeasure. In his judgment, nothing was quite right. He was surprised, however, to find that the hall was not nearly as long, from the front of the stage to the last row of seats, as he had imagined. It measured a hundred and twenty feet. Harris would have guessed that it was at least thirty feet longer than that. Like almost everyone who had been in the hall, he had been the victim of an optical illusion. The auditorium was wide in back, and it tapered toward the stage; the ceiling was high in back and sloped down in flat steps. These converging lines created a false impression of great length. Harris also noted that the building's steel skeleton, hidden by the auditorium's walls, formed a rectangle, just as wide in front as in back.

In the course of a second after-breakfast meeting, on December 10th, Harris told Ames what he had concluded. He discussed the hall one part at a time, beginning with the ceiling. Actually it had two ceilings, for, in the course of the 1969 remodelling, a new ceiling had been installed below the original one. But Harris was discussing the new ceiling only. Its shape was not good, Harris said, because it was essentially flat—a series of smooth plywood surfaces—and it was also too light in weight. It was not a good sound diffuser, for it absorbed some of the low frequencies. Harris thought it would have to come down. Then, the basic shape of the hall was strange—not rectangular but curved, like a Coca-Cola bottle—and the faces of the very long side balconies presented a pair of large concave surfaces. Such surfaces either cause echoes or concentrate sound in one area at the expense of other areas and so create dead spots. Some large concave surfaces can be rescued by putting bumps all over them, but the side-balcony faces needed bumps far bigger than they could accommodate. The side balconies, Harris believed, would have to be removed. As for the side walls, he did not approve of the way they were constructed, and he regarded their shape as wrong—like the ceiling, they were not diffusing sound properly. The best thing to do with the side walls, Harris thought, would be to get rid of them. The rear wall, which was also curved, was creating a concave-surface set of problems of its own. The rear wall would also have to be eliminated. The profile of the concrete floor, as it was shown in the drawings, was "far from optimal," as Harris put it. Part of it needed to be chopped away. Part of it needed to be raised by the addition of more concrete. But even then, Harris said, the floor would still be concrete, and in his opinion a wooden floor was essential to a good concert hall. The concrete floor, with its profile corrected, could serve as a foundation for a wooden floor, with an air space between the concrete and the wood. Though not much, Harris's verdict on the floor was the nicest thing he had to say about the hall.

Having demolished the ceiling, the side balconies, the side walls, the rear wall, and all but part of the floor, Harris had only the stage left. The shape of the stage, he explained to Ames, was acoustically undesirable; it was constructed in such a way that it absorbed a lot of the orchestra's low-frequency bass tones. The stage, Harris thought, would best be done away with, too.

Ames asked about the idea of moving the orchestra forward.

"That would improve things a little bit," Harris

said. "If you could do it without spending any money on it, I'd say go ahead. The trouble is that there is no way of fixing this or that. There are too many things to be fixed. The acoustical faults are too fundamental. The only way is to demolish the hall—tear it down, right back to the steel columns, and build a new one."

"The difficulty there," Ames said, "is that we don't have the money."

"In that case, I'd advise against your doing anything," Harris said. "No matter what you do, it will cost a lot of money, and the improvement, if any, will not be worth it."

While Harris had given Ames (and the City of New York) his very best counsel, he had taken no pleasure in saying what he had said. He had told the exact truth as he perceived it, and he had told it in a dramatic way —demolishing the hall before Ames's eyes—in the hope that Ames, Mazzola, Moseley, and Fisher would be convinced by the pedagogical device. In technical terms, the truth was considerably more complicated: the hall's dryness, or lack of reverberation, and its dead spots were the end result of a multiplicity of acoustical faults—things not done as well as things done wrong—that added up to an incurable condition, which was revealed by diagrams of the shape of the hall's sound-decay rate.

Students at Columbia who have successfully completed either of Harris's courses in acoustics—Architectural Acoustics (A-4128) or Experimental Acoustics (E-4495)—are keenly aware of the shape of the curves that show up on such diagrams ("decay-curve shape" is the phrase they use) because Harris goes out of his way to stress the fact that unshapely curves are a pitfall

for the concert-hall acoustician. Many of his students
have spent hours in the acoustics laboratory, learning
how to measure reverberation, plot the decay rate on
graph paper, appreciate its fine points, and analyze
imperfections when they appear. Harris's lectures are
mostly given in the Engineering School Building, at
the northeast corner of the campus, where 120th
Street and Amsterdam Avenue intersect. The lecture
room at the east end of the third floor, adjoining Harris's research laboratory, has a projector that he uses
frequently. His projection of an ideal sound-decay
curve (he calls it a curve, although it is more nearly a
squiggly straight line) for an ideal concert hall looks
like this:

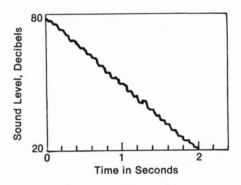

Harris's picture shows quite a loud sound (eighty
decibels) dying away to a very slight sound (twenty
decibels) in the course of two seconds, and, inciden-
tally, it portrays the definition of reverberation time—
the time required for a specific sound level to die away
by sixty decibels. In the case of this imaginary concert
hall, the reverberation time is two seconds. A full orchestra at its loudest can boom a chord louder than
ninety decibels, but it would seldom want to; that's

about the level of the sound inside an I.R.T. subway car going full speed. A young concertgoer—that is, one with acute hearing—could hear a sound softer than twenty decibels in a perfectly quiet room. But music at twenty decibels—as soft as the sound of leaves rustling—would not be audible at all in a concert hall, because the combined noises of air rushing out of the ventilators and the audience's breathing would drown it out.

Harris's teaching point in showing the picture, however, is to depict a decay curve of ideal smoothness: the squiggles in the line are the smallest that an acoustical consultant could dream of, for they indicate that the sound dies away evenly, without wide, erratic fluctuations back and forth between soft and loud. The sound gets softer steadily and at an even rate. To emphasize his point, Harris projects a picture of a horribly unsmooth decay curve:

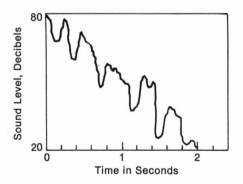

"If you should get a decay curve like that, the audience would be wretched," Harris tells his classes. "The human ear naturally prefers smooth decay. But in such a hall a tone would get softer and louder, still softer and then louder again—an erratic warble. The

music would sound terrible. And there is an interesting corollary: you, as the acoustician, would know that
some places in the auditorium were getting a lot more
sound than others. The rule is, the smoother the decay
curve the more uniform the sound pressure throughout the hall. And that's most important. You don't
want dead spots. You don't want good seats and bad
seats. You want all the seats to be good."

Then Harris explains a second decay-curve abomi-
nation, the "double slope." "Suppose the rate of
decay is uneven," he says. "Suppose at first the sound
dies away rapidly, and then, after perhaps a fraction of
a second, it dies away less rapidly. Then you get a
picture like this:

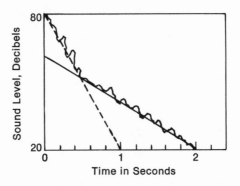

"The ear listens to the very rapid decay at first, and
interprets it as meaning that the reverberation time is
short," he continues. "The ear is tricked, because in
fact, after levelling off, the tone here is going to take
two seconds to decay sixty decibels, as in the first
picture. The ear has the impression that the reverberation time is short—as if it were just a little more than
one second—and that the hall is a rather dead one. In
other words, while the reverberation *time* is important,

the *shape* of the decay curve is equally important. It must be smooth. The crucial things to avoid are wide fluctuations and a double slope."

Harris goes on to explain that the way to achieve a smooth decay curve is to fill the hall with diffusing elements, so that the sound, as it bounces off the ceiling, the walls, the balcony fronts, and all the other interior surfaces, is scattered in every direction. (The heads of the audience are good diffusers, so a concert sounds better when it is sold out.) The famous concert halls of the past achieved excellent diffusion with deeply coffered and ornamented ceilings, crystal chandeliers, niches, cornices, friezes, extravagances of ornamental plastering, columns, windows, doors, cherubs, busts, and statues. Symphony Hall in Boston, the first concert hall in the world designed with the help of an acoustical scientist—Professor Wallace Clement Sabine, of the Harvard physics faculty—achieves part of its excellent diffusion with eighteen heroic replicas of Greek and Roman statues on pedestals in niches around the walls above the second balcony. The hall was built in 1900, and at the time the statues seemed a little splashy to Bostonians, but Sabine insisted that they were an acoustic necessity, and the chief architect, Charles F. McKim, of McKim, Mead and White, not only loved statues but suspected that Sabine knew his business. Since the acoustics of Symphony Hall, by common agreement, are wonderful, the statues no longer seem splashy to Bostonians.

In addition to being plentiful, a concert hall's diffusing elements should be of a variety of sizes, ranging from a few inches to twelve feet or more, in order to scatter high notes, with short wavelengths; middle-scale notes, with middle-sized wavelengths; and low notes, with long wavelengths. If a tone is to be diffused efficiently, the size of the diffusing obstacle must be comparable to the tone's wavelength. If, on the other hand, the wavelength exceeds the size of the obstacle by a good deal, it ignores the obstacle instead of bouncing off it in a new direction. Thus, a one-foot bump on a wall would not be a suitable diffuser for a middle-C tone, because the wavelength of middle C is a bit more than four feet, and it would be even less efficient for the C below middle C, whose wavelength is more than eight feet. The C two octaves below middle C, with a sixteen-foot wavelength, would take a two-foot bump in stride, so to speak. A two-foot bump, however, would diffuse the C an octave above middle C (wavelength, two feet) quite well. While high tones are diffused more easily than deep bass tones, a concert hall should have plenty of small diffusing obstacles as well as large ones. The busy ornamental plastering on oldfashioned coffered ceilings—acanthus leaves, egg-and-dart designs, and all sorts of other ridges and curlicues, their depth measurable in inches—were excellent short-wavelength diffusers, scattering the highest notes every which way.

A root trouble with Avery Fisher Hall in 1974 was with diffusion. There was not enough of it, and so the decay curve's fluctuations were irregular instead of smooth; moreover, the initial decay rate was too fast, resulting in a double slope. The sound of the orchestra was unevenly distributed—considerably more here, considerably less there—and, on the whole, the room seemed dead.

On December 18th, Harris and Ames met at Harris's apartment for a third conference. Ames and his three colleagues had been mulling over Harris's advice, and were completely agreed that doing nothing was an unacceptable solution. They were uneasy about the idea of demolishing the hall completely and starting over, although that had been suggested before, not always in jest. Fisher's instincts told him that complete rebuilding was probably required, but neither Fisher nor Ames nor Mazzola nor Moseley—nor Harris, for that matter—could guess how much it would cost. In any event, they had decided to scrap the orchestra-forward idea, and Ames wanted to find out whether Harris would act as acoustical consultant in case Lincoln Center should find the money to build a brand-new hall inside the old building.

Harris had half expected the question. He was confident that a fine new hall could be built within Avery Fisher Hall because the plans had shown that there was space within the upright girders for a rectangular hall almost matching the size and shape of three extraordinarily good concert halls that he had recently designed: the Great Hall at the Krannert Center for the Performing Arts, at the University of Illinois, in Champaign-Urbana (Max Abramovitz was the architect), which was completed in 1969; the Concert Hall at the John F. Kennedy Center for the Performing Arts, in Washington, which was completed in 1971; and Orchestra Hall, in Minneapolis, for the Minnesota Orchestra, which had just opened, mostly to critical raves, on October 21, 1974. These three halls had something besides Harris in common: in size and shape they all resembled Symphony Hall in Boston, which, in turn, resembled the Neues Gewandhaus in Leipzig, Germany—built in 1884 and destroyed during the Second World War—which had been part of

Professor Sabine's inspiration. Still, there is much
more to designing a good hall than imitating Boston's
version of the Neues Gewandhaus, and Harris, during
the first weeks of December, had formulated three
conditions that he believed would allow him the free-
dom to attend to everything.

"I'd consider doing the job if you will give me the
space I need," Harris told Ames. "That means that
everything comes down, right back to the girders.
And, second, if you will agree that acoustics will have
priority over aesthetics. If the architect and I should
disagree, I'd have to win the argument."

Ames did not say anything.

"And, third, if a new architect is to be selected, I'd
want you to retain Philip Johnson," Harris said, and he
went on to explain, "I am a difficult man to work with,
but Johnson and I get along well, and I know that we
could work together."

Ames, an admirer of Johnson's work, was amazed by
Harris's last condition. Ames had always believed—
Johnson, among others, had told him so—that *Johnson*
was difficult. If Harris considered Johnson easy to
work with, how difficult could Harris be? Ames went
back to Lincoln Center's offices to convey Harris's
terms to his colleagues.

Harris's confidence in his ability to collaborate with
Philip Johnson—and with John Burgee, Johnson's
partner in the firm of Johnson/Burgee—was solidly
based: they had all been collaborating for more than
a year on a concert hall for the National Center for the
Performing Arts in Bombay, India. The drawings were
finished, and a little of the construction work had been
done, but the completion date for the hall was indefinite. Harris and Johnson had worked together easily,

although in the beginning, Johnson had anticipated trouble. Harris had been thrust upon Johnson, and that fact alone might have caused some ruffling of feathers, for ordinarily, on an auditorium job, the architect retains an acoustical consultant, if he feels he needs one, and thus the architect is the consultant's boss. In the case of the Bombay concert hall, Johnson got the commission and was told soon afterward by his client, Jamshed Bhabha, acting for India's National Center for the Performing Arts, that the acoustical consultant was to be Cyril Harris. (Mr. Bhabha had just attended a performance at the Kennedy Center, and felt that the sound of Kennedy was precisely what Bombay wanted.) Johnson was dismayed. In 1964, Johnson and Harris had worked together on a small job—the board of trustees' room in the east wing of the Museum of Modern Art, here in New York—and, Johnson remembered, the personal chemistry had been less than perfect; Harris had been fussy about his acoustical suggestions, or so Johnson had thought. Still, as Johnson recalled not long ago, he and Burgee wanted the Bombay commission, even if they had to accept Harris. In next to no time, Johnson realized to his pleasure that Harris, though stubborn about acoustics, admired Johnson for being stubborn about aesthetics. "The better the architect, the harder the acoustical consultant has to work, and that's as it should be," Harris has said.

Harris admired Johnson's taste. Johnson, for his part, was impressed by Harris's detailed knowledge of architectural technology. The two men found that they could communicate in a kind of high-velocity verbal shorthand, or, on occasion, by saying hardly anything at all and drawing sketches on a scratch pad. "It

is partly because we share each other's prejudices,"
Johnson once remarked. "We are both fond of classic
shapes and traditional materials, and are not afraid to
admit it. And then, we get along well because Cyril
understands everything I say about architecture, and
I don't understand a word of what he says about
acoustics."

January, 1975: Some time passed before Harris next
heard from Ames. Harris suspected that the cost of
complete rebuilding was more than Lincoln Center
could afford. But since, as always, Harris was working
at top speed on various professional pursuits, he had
next to no time left in his schedule for brooding about
Avery Fisher Hall. He was getting ready for his se-
cond-semester classes at Columbia. In the fall of 1974,
he had taken on the chairmanship of one of the School
of Architecture's three divisions, the Division of Architectural Technology, thus committing himself to an
extra burden of academic chores—weighing student
admissions, approving courses of study, reading master's-degree-thesis proposals, and the like. In addition, having been fascinated for some time by lexicog-
raphy and having recently completed his first
dictionary—a volume defining more than twenty thousand technical terms and entitled "Dictionary of Architecture and Construction"—he was working on another such volume, called "Historic Architecture
Sourcebook." Harris is a coauthor (with Vern O.
Knudsen) of "Acoustical Designing in Architecture,"
the most widely used textbook in the field, which has
been translated into French, Japanese, and Chinese
(the last is a pirated edition); he is the editor of and
a contributor to another major acoustics text, "Hand-

Cyril M. Harris on the stage of the rebuilt Avery Fisher Hall.

April, 1976: Press conference on the Grand Promenade. The speakers, from left to right, are Mazzola, Fisher, Ames (standing), Harris, Johnson, Burgee, and Moseley.

*Left:* Demolition begins by removing the balcony lights.
*Above:* June, 1976: The rear balconies are partly torn down.

Superintendent Ernest Benzoni (right, with walkie-talkie), and Project Manager Eugene McGovern.

Mid-September: Construction is proceeding on all levels.

Plastering the ceiling.

No two flat surfaces of the finished ceiling are exactly parallel.

The opening night concert is two weeks away.

The auditorium has taken shape, but a lot of gold leaf has not yet been applied.

October 13, 1976: At the end of the first rehearsal, Harris and Ames were eager to know the orchestra's reaction.

October 19, 1976: The Opening Concert. From the right front: Mr. and Mrs. Amyas Ames, Mr. and Mrs. Avery Fisher, Mr. and Mrs. Cyril Harris, Mrs. Moss Hart, and Lord Drogheda.

The Orchestra plays "The Star-spangled Banner."

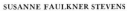

book of Noise Control," and a co-editor (with the late Charles E. Crede) of the three-volume "Shock and Vibration Handbook," which runs to two thousand and twenty-seven pages; and he has written or collaborated on more than fifty technical papers for various scientific publications, such as the *Journal of the Acoustical Society of America* and the *Journal of the Audio Engineering Society.* Nevertheless, as an author-editor, Harris had never had as much fun as he was getting out of writing dictionaries. For the "Historic Architecture Sourcebook" he was conferring with thirty or forty specialists in the United States and abroad, and filling up box after box of three-by-five file cards with alphabetized names and architectural terms, plus definitions, and—perhaps the most fun of all—assembling an alphabetized collection of more than ten thousand pictures, mostly line drawings and engravings, from which he expected to select perhaps twenty-one hundred illustrations. Harris had found that dictionary-making has a practical advantage for a busy man—the portability of materials. He now customarily carries a handful of his file cards in his pocket or in a black leather dispatch case, and, given an idle moment or two, fishes one out and works at polishing a definition.

Harris was born in Detroit on June 20, 1917, and his father, Dr. Bernard O. Harris, who was a successful general practitioner, died in the 1918 influenza epidemic. Three years later, Mrs. Harris, who had been a schoolteacher, decided to take Cyril, her only child, to California. In Hollywood, where they settled, Mrs. Harris obtained an insurance broker's license, and she has been in the insurance business there ever since.

(Now in her middle seventies, she claims that she retired in 1970, but she still goes to her office and looks after the insurance needs of a few old clients.) Harris remembers Hollywood in the twenties with great fondness. His mother enrolled him in a nursery school called the Wee Tots Villa, and, like countless other American mothers at the time, made him wear his hair in the Dutch-boy style popularized by Jackie Coogan in Charlie Chaplin's film "The Kid." Although Cyril Harris, who had a thin face and high cheekbones, did not look at all like Jackie Coogan, his first paying job, at the age of five and a half, was as a movie actor in a Hal Roach "Our Gang" comedy. To his regret, Harris has never seen the film, and all he can remember is that a lot of custard pies were thrown. Neither he nor his mother was interested in his becoming a child film star, but Harris, as he grew up, became increasingly attracted to the studios because of the many fascinating gadgets they contained. The junior high school he attended was across the street from the Warner Brothers studio, which was pioneering in the new sound-reproduction techniques for talking films, and at that time Harris was becoming fascinated by electronics and was building radios, amplifiers, and radio transmitters. He also worked at odd jobs after school, and whenever he got onto the Warner Brothers lot as a delivery boy or messenger he spent as much time inspecting the electronic equipment as he dared. Harris discovered that, rather than risk spoiling a sound track on account of weak batteries in the sound equipment, the Warner technicians used new storage batteries even when there was still quite a lot of life in the old ones. He was able to buy the used batteries, which might have cost ten or fifteen dollars new, for ten or fifteen cents, and he used them to power an amateur broadcasting station of his own, W6IJE, which he built while he was attending Holly-wood High School.

Harris sometimes thought about making movie sound-reproduction work his career, but when he en-tered the University of California at Los Angeles, in 1934, he decided to follow his father into the medical profession. In the premedical course, he discovered, to his dismay, that he despised chemistry. Realizing that he did not care much about becoming a doctor after all, he had himself tested by a Los Angeles apti-tude-testing firm, which informed him that business administration was his natural forte. That sounded almost as bad as chemistry, so Harris decided to switch to mathematics and bone up on the study of statistics, which might be useful in business, in case the apti-tude-testing people turned out to be right. As a mathe-matics major, Harris was required to minor in physics, and in his senior year he came upon acoustics, the science dealing with the ways sound is produced and transmitted and what its effects are. He had always been a good student, but now he exploded with aca-demic excitement, and raced through almost all the acoustics literature available in the Greater Los An-geles area. He discovered that a large part of the theo-retical work in the field had been done quite recently, which pleased him, because it suggested there might be a lot left to do. He was thrilled by the multitude of interrelated acoustical problems. Abandoning all thoughts of a career in business administration, Harris went on to U.C.L.A.'s graduate school to work for a Ph.D. in physics, but even before he had earned his M.A. he knew he wanted to transfer to the Massachusetts Institute of Technology and study with Professor Philip McCord Morse, whose technical papers and books Harris greatly admired.

M.I.T. gave Harris a research fellowship and then a teaching fellowship to help pay for his studies. He arrived in Cambridge in 1940, and, with the onset of the Second World War, the government became interested in acoustical research, so from the end of his first semester at M.I.T. until he received his doctorate Harris was also employed in research on devices such as bombs and mines with acoustical triggers. Although by 1945 he was an expert in that field, his doctoral thesis was not on the subject of weapons. With Professor Morse as his intellectual guide, and with room acoustics and acoustical materials as his particular interest, Harris did his thesis on "Application of the Wave Theory of Room Acoustics to the Measurement of Acoustic Impedence."

At the time Harris received his doctorate, Dr. Harvey Fletcher, one of the great figures in acoustics history, was the director of physical research at the Bell Telephone Laboratories, in Murray Hill, New Jersey, which was at that time the leading acoustical-research center in the country. Fletcher offered him a job. The war had not yet ended, and Bell was deeply involved in military research, so Harris started out working on a torpedo that would home in on the noise made by an enemy ship. After the war, he turned to more peaceful matters: a point-source loudspeaker to be used with a point microphone for high-quality sound reproduction, porous screens and how they absorb sound, and speech synthesis. The last project involved developing a way of assembling the component

sounds of human speech on one magnetic tape, printing them in various sequences on another tape, and
coming up with a voice talking, if in slightly inhuman
tones. Harris became the co-inventor of a talking typewriter (Bell Laboratories owns the patent), which
could prove useful if anyone wanted his computer to
talk instructions instead of printing them out. Bell
Laboratories was as great, scientifically, as Harris had
anticipated, and he stayed there for six years. Yet as
time went on he felt slightly constrained, because, as
an employee of a profit-making firm, he was supposed
to stick to business, and although Harris was intensely
interested in the research he did, he sometimes wished
he were free to wander off in whatever direction he
chose. He also discovered that, after his M.I.T. experience, he missed teaching.

In November, 1948, at a party in New York City,
Harris met Ann Schakne, a Hunter College graduate
who had gone on to Radcliffe for an M.A. in English
and had just become a junior editor at a publishing
house. Miss Schakne was dark-haired, very pretty, and
lively, and she and Harris quickly discovered a common bond: she, too, had gone to college planning to
be a physician and chemistry had changed her mind.
She was another man's date at the party, but Harris
called her up the following day, and less than a year
later, on July 12, 1949, they were married.

A year and a half after that, Harris quit his job at Bell
Laboratories and Mrs. Harris quit hers, and they sailed
for England, third class on the Île-de-France, without
any plan except to stay abroad as long as their money
lasted. Over the next seventeen months, Harris held
two jobs: a consulting assignment from the London
branch of the United States Office of Naval Research

to travel throughout Europe for six months inspecting acoustics laboratories, followed immediately by a job teaching acoustics, on a Fulbright Exchange Program lectureship, at the Technical University of Delft, Holland. What brought the Harrises back to the United States, in mid-1952, was the birth of a son, Nicholas. They also have a daughter, Katherine (known as Katie), three years younger. When the family returned to America, Harris fancied the idea of going back to California, but his wife could not imagine that anyone would think seriously of living anywhere except in New York City. Ann Harris won the point, because Columbia made her husband an offer more attractive than anything he received from California. Harris soon took up his duties as an associate professor of electrical engineering there, and before long his wife went to work as an editor at Harper, where she still is.

When Harris arrived on the campus, Columbia had no acoustics-research laboratory worthy of the name, and no money to build one. Harris built his own. With what is now called a little "seed money"—in this case a research contract on stereophonic sound from the late Major Edwin H. Armstrong, the inventor of FM radio—Harris set up a small lab in the basement of the philosophy building. From that starting point, by hustling for other research contracts, and by spending as much money as he could justify on equipment, Harris acquired a good laboratory on the university's behalf. He ran out of space in the basement, and moved to the old Sheffield Farms building, owned by Columbia, on 125th Street, not far from the Hudson. By the late fifties, he had promoted so many contracts that he had assembled a research group of eight engineers and four technicians. After the Seeley W. Mudd building was finished, in 1961, Harris moved all the laboratory equipment from the former milk-bottling plant to the main campus.

The research Harris has done, sometimes with the help of graduate students, covers a multitude of subjects. Following up the work he started at Bell Laboratories, he has worked on speech analysis, speech synthesis, the effects of noise on hearing, and speaker identification. Harris called my attention to the acoustical accuracy of the explanation in Alexander Solzhenitsyn's novel "The First Circle" of the limitations on identification by voice. Voices are not like fingertips, in spite of exaggerated publicity to the contrary about voiceprints. It is possible to identify a speaker with a high degree of probability, Harris says, but someone else may have a voice so similar that even the most detailed analysis, processed by a computer, cannot distinguish between them. Among musical instruments of which Harris has done acoustical studies, in addition to the bagpipe, are the French horn and the classical guitar; he has investigated the acoustical properties of carpets; and for one summer during the Korean war he worked at the University of Michigan on acoustical means of gathering battlefield intelligence. His most extensive research, financed primarily by the National Aeronautics and Space Administration and the Office of Naval Research, has been a series of studies on sound absorption in air at differing temperatures and humidities, and on the effect of humidity on the speed with which sound travels in air—studies that he began in the early nineteen-sixties and pursued until 1971. It took two years just to construct the main piece of equipment—a spherical metal reverberation chamber about five feet in diameter in which the temperature and humidity could be perfectly controlled. Its reverberation time is five minutes, the longest of any enclosure in the world. Harris's data are more accurate than any previously obtained. A lot of sound is absorbed in air, and knowing exactly how much is absorbed is essential in measuring aircraft noise, for instance, or in designing the acoustics for a big concert hall. Although the effect of humidity on the speed of sound in air is exceedingly small, the change in velocity can change the direction of sound waves in the atmosphere. No one had ever measured it before in a laboratory. That, says Harris, was the fascinating challenge. It also turned out to have practical applications.

Harris had not heard from Ames because Ames, Mazzola, Moseley, and Fisher were in the process of deciding whether or not to go ahead. While their informal committee was so powerful that it hardly needed to consult anybody, consultation was the diplomatic thing, and there were scores of people to be spoken with, starting with the thirty-four members of Lincoln Center's board of directors. Then the board of directors of the Philharmonic needed to be brought into the picture, along with the members of the orchestra; its current conductor, Pierre Boulez; its managing director, Albert K. Webster; and Webster's staff. The members of the Lincoln Center Council, representing all the organizations in the agglomeration—the Metropolitan Opera, the New York City Ballet, the Film Society, the Juilliard School, the New York Shakespeare Festival, the New York City Opera, the Chamber Music Society, and the New York Public Library—had to be alerted. (There were twelve members, including Moseley and Mazzola, who already knew what was going on, and one other member who didn't need to be tipped off; he was Mark Schubart, director of Lincoln Center Institute, whose office is close to Ames's and Mazzola's, and who was being kept informed of developments as they occurred.) Rebuilding would be bound to make a mess of the Plaza, to mention the least of the problems that the Harris proposal could create, so it was only polite to tell everybody who might be affected what was being contemplated.

From the moment Harris had counselled rebuilding, thus opening up an array of possibilities, Fisher and Moseley had been thinking about the kind of sound that would suit the Philharmonic best. Fisher mentioned a "perfect" hall—a word that Harris shies away from. The best that can be achieved is, as Harris expresses it, "a hall of acoustical excellence," and he specifies, *"for symphonic music,"* because such excellence requires a single purpose. The Festspielhaus in Bayreuth, built by the composer Richard Wagner for music by Richard Wagner, may be the only true single-purpose auditorium in the world, but it is an opera house, not a concert hall. A concert hall is not designed to be used for opera, light opera, musical comedy, theatre, or lectures, but since orchestras play all kinds of music, the acoustics of the hall should enhance every kind. Sometimes the full orchestra plays, sometimes it is reduced in size. Orchestras often play concertos, and it is crucial that the solo instrument not be drowned out by the accompaniment. Some works, too, are scored for vocal soloists and chorus. Orchestras perform the music of several centuries' worth of composers. Some orchestras, including the Philhar-

monic, play to full houses; others are lucky to fill as
many as eighty-five per cent of the seats. A concert hall
of "acoustical excellence" must work well for that ex-
tended range of possibilities. As a practical matter,
Fisher's use of the word "perfect" was supposed to
mean merely "the best concert hall in the world."

Fisher and Moseley, whose experience as a concert
pianist and as a soloist with the orchestra made him
especially aware of the musicians' perspective, along
with David M. Keiser, who had been the chairman of
the board of the Philharmonic before Ames, and was
chairman of the board of the Juilliard School and a
pillar of strength on the Lincoln Center board, had
been flying around the United States listening to concerts, checking to see whether they liked any hall better than Symphony Hall in Boston, which they all knew
well and admired. (The Grosser Musikvereinssaal in
Vienna and the Concertgebouw in Amsterdam had
their partisans, but not in this triumvirate.) On this
search they had found two such halls. One was Harris's three-year-old Concert Hall at the Kennedy Center and the other was Harris's brand-new Orchestra
Hall in Minneapolis. All things considered, they preferred both to Boston.

Money was still a problem to the committee, but not
nearly as great a problem as it had been, because
Fisher had seen a possible solution. His ten-million-
dollar gift to Lincoln Center in 1973, a capital fund for
"maintaining, operating, and improving" the hall, had
been in the form of a pledge. He had already delivered
about five million dollars of this endowment, and, according to his plan, the remaining five million was to
be paid in installments through 1978. Fisher thought
he might instead give the entire balance to Lincoln

Center right away. That would provide Lincoln Center
with cash to pay for the rebuilding, although it would
mean that Lincoln Center would be dipping into capital. The questions were, how much dipping into capital would be required, and would the State Supreme
Court—which keeps an eye on earmarked gifts to non-
profit organizations—understand and approve the notion that the maintenance, operation, and improvement of the hall depended upon its insides being
demolished? Fisher, a handsome, not quite white-
haired man of sixty-eight, who speaks with a soft,
husky voice, took the view that things could be worked
out. His parents had arrived in New York from Russia
a few years before Avery was born. Theirs was a large,
prosperous, and extremely musical family; nearly everybody played an instrument, and young Avery studied the violin with Sam Franko, who in *his* youth had
studied with Joseph Joachim and Henri Vieuxtemps.
The Fishers could, and did, field a string quartet without calling in any outsiders; chamber music became
Avery's great enthusiasm, and it still is. By Fisher's
own reckoning, he is no more than a "good amateur"
violinist, but he has been privately playing in string
quartets and small chamber orchestras regularly for
forty years, where he has held his own with professional musicians. In order to earn his living, after
graduating from New York University's Washington
Square College in 1929, Fisher went into advertising
—graphics was his interest—and then into book designing, for Dodd, Mead. He became well known as a
designer, and did many of Dodd, Mead's books, including Edwin Way Teale's "Grassroot Jungles."
Early in 1976, Fisher designed the seventy-seven-year-
old naturalist's latest book, "The American Seasons,"

which Dodd, Mead published in October; and Fisher
was hired, on a free-lance basis, at Teale's suggestion.
According to Fisher, Teale asked his publishers,
"Whatever became of that good young designer,
Avery Fisher?" Then, in 1937, Fisher went into business for himself, but not into the graphics business.
Besides music, he had another hobby—designing and
building high-fidelity sound equipment for himself
and his friends. He decided to start a company and see
whether there was any money in manufacturing and
selling his radios and record-players on a commercial
scale. The Fisher Radio Corporation did extremely
well. He sold it, in 1969, to the Emerson Electric Company for thirty-one million dollars, and since then
most of his energy and a lot of his money has gone into
music—especially music at Lincoln Center, where he
is active on three boards of directors (the Center's, the
Philharmonic's, and the Chamber Music Society's),
and in the Green Mountains of Vermont, where he is
a trustee of the Marlboro Music Festival. Fisher, in
short, was anything but a gullible patron. He had been
concerned with acoustics for as long as he could remember, and had made his fortune out of that concern: furthermore, given a good fiddle, he was person-
ally prepared to demonstrate how a violin should
sound.

No one knew within a million dollars or two how
much demolition and rebuilding would cost. In 1962,
the construction of Philharmonic Hall had cost about
eighteen million dollars. In cubic feet, the auditorium
itself accounted for only a quarter of the building's
total interior space, with the rest occupied by promenade spaces, the Philharmonic offices and board
room, locker and instrument-storage rooms, elevators, passageways, stairwells, lavatories, rehearsal

rooms, and the like, but no one imagined that the answer to the big question in 1975 was eighteen million divided by four—although, as things worked out, four and a half million would have been about right. Tearing down a concert hall inside a building had never been done before, and it promised to be expensive. (One could hardly whack at the walls with a steel ball swinging on the end of a cable.) Besides, 1975 dollars were not 1962 dollars. There was a mitigating factor, though, which was that the construction industry in New York City was in a slump, so it was possible that hungry contractors would submit low bids. Of the many other unknowns, the greatest was the new hall's design. What were Harris and Johnson/Burgee going to think up? There had to be some limit on the fraction of the ten million dollars that it would be prudent for Lincoln Center to spend. Before going as far as signing contracts, Ames, Mazzola, Moseley, and Fisher needed a rational cost estimate.

February, 1975: Harris and Johnson began to work on a new Avery Fisher Hall. In principle, neither acoustical consultants nor architects work on speculation, but somehow an exception seemed suitable in this particular case. Members of Ames's staff are given to saying that Ames "can persuade anybody to do anything," and they may be right. Anyway, in late January, Ames had asked Harris and Johnson to make some preliminary plans. The idea was to go just far enough with the design to be able to describe it verbally in considerable detail—especially the construction niceties—without actually designing the hall. (The finished design, portrayed in architectural drawings and augmented by a volume of precise specifications, could keep Harris, Johnson, and Burgee, and

Johnson/Burgee's draftsmen and consulting engineers, busy for the better part of a year.) The idea was for Harris and Johnson to get in touch with Carl Morse, a construction consultant and the head of the Morse/Diesel Construction Corporation, and tell Morse a whole lot about what they were going to design—on the assumption that they were going to design it—so that Morse and the experts on his staff could translate the concept into dollars. Then Lincoln Center would have a figure, which it might or might not be able to afford.

Harris and Johnson, within the first few minutes of their first conversation, found that they were agreed on many points. For one thing, the hall would be rectangular. Johnson knew from past association that as a rule Harris would always suggest a rectangle for a concert hall, although Bombay is the rule-testing exception. The hall there is to be used primarily not for Western but for Indian music, which needs a shorter reverberation time, and requires that the audience be as close as possible to the stage, in order to see the facial expressions of the musicians, especially when the percussionist on the hand drums and the sitar player engage in their exchanges. Therefore, Bombay is to be shaped rather like a Greek theatre—an arrangement that puts the last rows closer to the stage. For Western symphonic music, Harris likes the traditional rectangular shape. Once a rectangle was agreed on, Harris and Johnson could come close to predicting its dimensions—something like ninety feet by a hundred and twenty feet, not counting the stage. The auditorium could not be much bigger, because the upright girders set the limits; it could not be much smaller, because the hall's seating capacity, which was then two thousand eight hundred and thirty six, had to remain nearly the same. (It is now two thousand seven hundred and forty-two.) They discussed the balconies. Harris avoids deep balconies, because it is hard to attain even sound distribution beneath a deep overhang; he also likes to keep the opening between tiers as large as possible, so the sound can enter and bounce out again. They decided on three shallow balconies, with shallow boxes extending forward on both sides all the way to the front of the house.

Harris and Johnson met a number of times, usually with John Burgee joining their discussions, and usually at the Johnson/Burgee offices, high in the Seagram Building (which Mies van der Rohe and Johnson designed), on Park Avenue, with a magnificent view of the East River. They talked about what sort of facings the balconies might have, but they didn't try to go very far with that subject, since whatever the facings were to be, the cost would not be much affected. They talked at greater length about the ceiling, concluding that it would be intricate, because it would provide a major part of the hall's diffusion for all wavelengths, and that it would be heavy plaster, to minimize sound absorption. They agreed that the hall must contain lots of wood: a wooden floor for the auditorium, a wooden floor for the stage, wooden panelling on the walls, and a wooden shell behind the orchestra to help give its sound a powerful throw. By about the third or fourth conference, Harris, Johnson, and Burgee had agreed on a rather surprising idea: the stage would be framed by a great rectangular proscenium, less for acoustical than for aesthetic reasons: it would serve as a visual magnet, drawing all attention to the musicians onstage.

Having reached many such decisions, and having
arrived at a point where they could begin to envision
the new Avery Fisher Hall, Harris, Johnson, and Burgee felt pleased. Harris always thinks that the hall he
is working on is going to be a little better than any he
has done before. Each time, Harris believes, he
profits, if only slightly, from having built the previous
hall. Architecturally, Orchestra Hall in Minneapolis is
much more radical than Kennedy, because the most
conspicuous diffusing elements of the former design
are what seem to be huge cubes set into the ceiling and
cascading down the wall behind the stage; and, while
Harris could understand that such boldness might not
be to everyone's taste, he thought that the resultant
acoustics could not be faulted. Kennedy is more con-
servative visually; its diffusive elements in the ceiling
are concentric hexagonal patterns in coffered plaster,
augmented by diffusing chandeliers, and, while the
ceiling is intricate, it calls little attention to itself. But
Fisher preferred the *sound* of Kennedy to the sound of
Orchestra Hall. Harris agreed that the sounds were
not exactly alike, but he thought that the difference
was not significant. He pointed out that the sound of
the new Avery Fisher Hall would also be unique, because two halls with identical acoustics could be
achieved only if they were identical in every respect.
As for Johnson and Burgee, they also liked the way the
preliminary talks were going. They felt that the classic
shape of the hall and its straight lines were a delight,
and that what was evolving would express the traditional in contemporary terms—elegant, clean, dignified, and impressive, without a single Greek or
Roman statue on the premises.

The time had come to talk with Carl Morse. Morse

and several members of his staff joined Harris, Johnson, and Burgee at the Johnson/Burgee offices, and the group went over the imaginary hall part by part, discussing construction details rather than acoustical or architectural conceptions, and discussing them in terms of the work involved. For instance, Harris, Johnson, and Burgee told Morse that they had agreed that the floor of the auditorium, which would be about ten thousand square feet, should be made of oak three-quarters of an inch thick, nailed to three-quarter-inch plywood mounted on wooden two-by-fours over masonry supports, with a foot of air space underneath. Then they described the construction of the wood-panelled walls: the thickness of the panelling, and how it would be fastened on vertical strips of wood mounted on dense concrete blocks with compressed fibre glass filling the spaces between the concrete and the panelling. The walls would have a complexity of irregularities—indentations of assorted sizes every few feet. They talked about the ceiling, which in square feet would be approximately the same size as the floor. As far as construction materials and methods were concerned, the three men might almost have been describing Orchestra Hall, Kennedy, or, for that matter, Krannert. On and on they went, drawing occasional sketches, but mostly talking, while Morse and his staff took copious notes.

Then Morse and his people withdrew to their offices to make calculations on the basis of the information they had been given, and in doing so they added to the cost of the new hall the cost of demolishing the old one. (Demolition-cost estimates can be almost as tricky as building-cost estimates; while a structure is being torn down, any number of surprises may be encountered. And, indeed, in this case the wreckers discovered unexpected lumps of solid concrete under the auditorium's old floor, near the bases of the steel uprights.) Within a week or so, Morse had a total estimate. He told Ames what it was.

Ames called a meeting of the committee, and announced Morse's figure: three and a half million dollars.

"Well," said Avery Fisher, "I don't see anything wrong with that."

The thing that was wrong with three and a half million, as the actual bills, twenty months later, showed, was that it was too low by nearly a million and a half. But then, Ames, Mazzola, Moseley, and Fisher were well aware that preliminary estimates are invariably low, and they were relieved that the sum was not greater. They were all ready to gamble that much, and even somewhat more, on their belief that Harris and Johnson/Burgee could deliver "a hall of acoustical excellence." Fisher, who had had the least difficulty contemplating complete rebuilding, was the calmest of the four. He felt that Harris was a little prickly whenever anyone invaded his territory of expertise, as Fisher had done on one or two occasions, but he was greatly impressed by Harris's candor and passion for detail; they were both qualities that reminded Fisher of himself. Ames was not worried, either. He believed that Harris, on his "track record," as Ames called it, deserved Lincoln Center's trust, and, besides, Ames had developed a certain gut feeling that Harris was a man who would deliver what he promised. Moseley thought that Harris, having done Krannert, Kennedy, and Orchestra Hall, could do another just as good, and that that would be enough to rejoice the Philharmonic. As for Mazzola, he looks a bit like a gambler; he is a giant, with the face and style of a Roman emperor, and he is a gourmet, bon vivant, and high-powered business executive. Mazzola was the only member of the committee who had previously dealt with Harris, and then only on the telephone, but he had been impressed. The air-conditioning tower on the roof of the Metropolitan Opera House (another building for which Harris had been a consultant) had been making a racket. Though inaudible in the building, the noise was disturbing to people outside, on the Plaza level, where the fountain is. Mazzola's workmen had struggled to quiet it, to no avail, and finally Mazzola had phoned Harris. Like a patient calling a doctor, Mazzola described the symptoms. "Well, three or four things could be wrong," Harris had said, "but I can give you a list of corrections to try, in the order you ought to try them." Then Harris had dictated a brief list. Suggestion No. 3 had solved the problem completely. Mazzola had made a mental note that Harris was a man who knew what he was talking about. Mazzola also liked the notion, which Harris had stressed, that everything about the new hall would be time-tested—and some aspects would have been tested for three-quarters of a century. In Mazzola's file cabinets, just outside his office door, he keeps a folder labelled "Philharmonic Halls I Have Known," with the details of all the refurbishings the place had been through, and he was pleased to think that nothing of an experimental nature was in contemplation. Mazzola was ready to take the plunge.

By the middle of March, the committee's recommendation had been approved unanimously by the

board of the Philharmonic and the board of Lincoln
Center, with Ames presiding over both meetings; the
court's decision on allowing the use of Lincoln Center's endowment-fund maintenance money had been
handed down, and it was favorable; contracts had been
signed with Harris and Johnson/Burgee, finally recti-
fying their volunteer status. Lincoln Center's director
of public information, John O'Keefe, set up a press
conference for Tuesday the twenty-fifth. "It is clear
that something has to be done," Ames explained to
the assembled reporters. "We have to offer the best.
The reputation of Lincoln Center stands on it. We also
have a responsibility to the musicians who play in
Fisher Hall. We have great confidence in Dr. Harris
and Mr. Johnson, and we look forward to a hall equal
to any in the world."

April, 1975: Harris began attending Philharmonic
rehearsals, sitting with the orchestra wherever there
was an empty desk—for there was almost always at
least one. He wanted to find out exactly what the musicians meant when they complained, as they had for
over twelve years, that they could not hear properly
onstage. He also wanted to get to know them, individ-
ually and as a group. Among the people he hoped to
please, the musicians ranked very high. If in the end
the Philharmonic itself did not like the new hall, no
praise from the critics would make up for that failure.
Harris had sometimes sat in with other clients' orchestras, and he wanted to sit in with the Philharmonic as
often as possible. The fact that the West Side I.R.T.
connects Lincoln Center with Columbia University
enabled him to do this frequently.

After Harris sat through his first rehearsal with the

Philharmonic—he had found a seat in the trumpet section—the musicians recovered quickly from their initial surprise. At every break, Harris, walking out with them and chatting backstage, was deluged with questions about acoustics, which he was happy to answer, and was told of their problems, which were multitudinous. An orchestra member's lot, to hear the orchestra member tell it, is not a happy one. Harris recognized that most of their acoustical complaints had merit, and he intended to relieve them of as many of them as he could.

July, 1975: Work on the plans and specifications was proceeding. There had been no real gap between the preliminary plans and the beginning of work on the final plans, one endeavor having led directly into the other. All told, Harris, Johnson, and Burgee had been designing for about six months, and they hoped they had gone more than halfway. Every few days, Harris would go down to the Johnson/Burgee offices. Some of the conferences were short. (A few took place over the telephone.) Others were long. Whatever was decided would be translated into technical drawings, precise and to scale. Copies would be made, and one delivered to Harris. Harris would study the plan and consider how the detail fitted into the total acoustical scheme, and would perhaps make marks on the drawing, or make a few notes in the margins. Then the three men would meet again. Johnson and Burgee would look at the marks Harris had made, and ponder what Harris's idea would do to their concept of the architectural scheme. They would propose an alteration, perhaps, and yet another variation would evolve, which would be turned over to the draftsmen for a new drawing. So the process went, sometimes quickly but more often slowly. Nothing could be settled by itself and put aside, because where acoustics are concerned all parts of the auditorium are interdependent: a minor change in the size, shape, or construction of any detail could call for compensating changes in almost everything else.

While Avery Fisher Hall was going to look something like Kennedy, the differences were significant. Kennedy, for instance, is lit by eleven large crystal chandeliers, which contribute to its sound diffusion. Avery Fisher Hall was not going to have any chandeliers; instead, it would have rows of globes arranged on the ceiling in bands, running across it from one side to the other. Although these globes—along with rows of light bulbs on the undersides of the boxes and balconies—would provide some diffusion for short wavelengths, most of the longer-wavelength diffusion would have to be supplied by the sculptured surfaces of the ceiling, the irregularities of the side walls, and the balcony facings. The basic rectangles of the two halls were nearly identical, but Kennedy has fewer rows of seats, because it has eight feet of room for standees behind the last row in the orchestra. (Avery Fisher would have, at the rear corners of the topmost tier, two desks, with two seats at each, for students wishing to read scores.) In total cubic volume, including the stage as well as the auditorium, Avery Fisher would be about the same size as Kennedy—a little more than six hundred and sixty thousand cubic feet.

Professor Sabine had figured out, before he was consulted about Symphony Hall, that reverberation time increases with cubic volume and decreases as absorption increases, and in honor of Sabine's discovery the unit of measurement for sound absorption is the sabin, even as the measure of sound level, the bel —or, in its more frequently used fraction of ten, the decibel—honors Alexander Graham Bell. Harris had kept absorption at Kennedy extremely low, to give the auditorium liveness, and he knew he had to keep it extremely low at Avery Fisher. The clothes on a capacity audience absorb a great deal of sound, but capacity audiences are to be desired, not discouraged, and it was not Harris's place to urge the subscribers to wear very thin dresses or summer-weight suits. He did, however, suggest to Johnson and Burgee that the checking facilities be improved, in the hope that in winter most members of the audience would check their coats instead of holding them on their laps. This is no minor point. Few people realize that by checking their coats they help acoustics, but Harris tells of the managers of a good old auditorium who once called him up in distress because they thought their hall was somehow dying. That sounded unlikely. Harris questioned them closely and discovered that the hall still sounded all right in summer. Then, under his questioning, the hall's directors admitted that they had ripped out their coat checkroom. It was restored, and the hall sounded the way it used to.

Air is also absorptive, and its absorptive capacity varies as the temperature and humidity change. In addition to keeping Avery Fisher Hall comfortably air-conditioned, it was important to keep its relative humidity constant, at forty-five to fifty-five, for the sake of the orchestra's tonal balance. Harris wanted to eliminate all carpeting inside the hall except in the aisles, where it would be required to keep patrons from slipping and falling, and to muffle the noise of

their footsteps when they arrived late or departed
early. Carpet can be highly absorptive (as Harris's
paper on the subject, "The Acoustical Properties of
Carpet," had explained to readers of the *Journal of the
Acoustical Society of America* for November of 1955). He
recommended fairly non-absorptive, low-pile carpeting for the aisles. Johnson and Burgee envisioned the
auditorium as being antique white, for the most part,
trimmed with gold—gold velvet seats with oak backs,
gold balcony facings, gold lighting fixtures, and a gold
proscenium—and as having a dark wooden stage, to
contrast dramatically with the rest of the house. Harris
also stressed, as he had from the beginning of the
preliminary planning, how important it was to use
heavy building materials, along with construction
techniques that would maximize the structure's solid-
ity and rigidity—except for the floor of the auditorium
and the floor of the stage, where some flexibility was
wanted. Almost every material—even granite—ab-
sorbs some sound, if only an infinitesimal amount. But
by the use of high-density plaster and massive concrete wall blocks, with materials attached to one another very tightly, and by the use of a strong framework where a light framework might ordinarily suffice,
the amount of absorption could be kept to a minimum.

The ceiling, slightly more than ten thousand feet
square, was a battlefield, where acoustics, architectural design, and architectural technology fought to a
three-way accommodation. Johnson and Burgee felt
that the ceiling ought not to attract attention at the
expense of the stage. Harris agreed. Yet the ceiling
had to do a lot of work acoustically. It did not need to
be visually obtrusive, but it could hardly be simple.
With the smoothest of smooth decay curves ever in

mind, Harris required that the ceiling provide a multiplicity of diffusing obstacles of assorted sizes; that it be massive and rigid, to minimize absorption; and that it be solid, so that no sound could escape through holes or at the edges into the space above. The ceiling would be hung from the roof of the building on springmounted rods called isolators. The isolators were to prevent outside noise—vibrations in the structure of the outer building, or the roar of airplanes overhead—from penetrating the auditorium. If the roof shook, the ceiling would stay still. Each of the hundreds of isolator rods could support at least four hundred pounds of plaster on metal lath.

Harris suggested a ceiling studded with upsidedown pyramids. The Johnson/Burgee draftsmen prepared a sketch. It looked terrible—like a bat's-eye view of the Sigfried Line. Johnson pointed out that if the pyramids were broken up into their component planes they would look less obtrusive. Another set of drawings. Visually, the second concept was an improvement, and acoustically nothing had been lost, but the truth was that neither Johnson and Burgee nor Harris really liked it, and they told each other so, in their private code of grunts, pencil marks, and meaningful silences. While counting up was difficult, since the end of one concept carried over into the beginning of the next, the three men went through no fewer than twelve distinct versions of the ceiling design, and were beginning to think they almost had it.

August, 1975: The Department of Buildings of the New York City Housing and Development Administration had a monkey wrench in hand, ready to throw into the Harris-Johnson-Burgee machinery. New York can be proud of the fact that its building code, and especially the fire-prevention sections of the code, is as stringent as any in the nation. The Department of Buildings reviews plans for new public places before construction. For places of public assembly, such as concert halls, this review covers the finishing materials. Whenever Harris, Johnson, and Burgee were sufficiently agreed on certain construction details, they submitted them to the Department of Buildings, rather than wait to get all the plans for everything in final form. The department took a poor view of the new wooden floor—particularly of the air space between the concrete underpinning and the plywood on which the oak flooring would be mounted. The department felt that in case of fire that air space might be hazardous. Would it be possible, the department wondered, to place the plywood underflooring directly on the concrete instead of mounting it on supports? Acoustically, the answer was no. The floor almost matched the floors at Champaign-Urbana, Washington, and Minneapolis, which had all met the local codes without difficulty—although that was irrelevant. The acoustical function of the air space was to give the floor a certain amount of flexibility, so that it could vibrate, if only slightly, in response to the sound of the orchestra, and allow the members of the audience, with their feet on the floor, to be able to feel the music as well as hear it. The Department of Buildings suggested that the space be retained but filled with something nonflammable. The trouble there, Harris explained, was that filling in the space would change the acoustical value of the floor, and thus the acoustics of the entire hall. Could some material be cemented to the underside of the plywood which would fireproof the wood? Harris was not keen about that idea. "I do not like to gamble," he said. "I want to know in advance that I am going to win."

In the end, the impasse was broken. The air-conditioning system was to pull stale air out of the auditorium through holes in the floor. If smoke-detecting sensors could be installed near the exhaust fans, and some fire-resistant material installed below, but not touching, the plywood, the city code would be completely satisfied. Harris said that would have no effect on the acoustics one way or another.

November, 1975: Though Harris is a lexicographer, he seldom uses colorful words to describe the sound he hopes to achieve. Whenever he mentioned his acoustical goals to Johnson or Burgee, he spoke in value-free technical terms. Things were to be done for "diffusion" or "absorption" or "the reverberation time" or "dynamic range" or "smooth decay." The adjectives and adjectival phrases that music critics and musicians use to describe their concepts of good sound—such as "balanced," "blended," "bright," "brilliant," "colorful," "clear," "detailed," "distinct," "dynamic," "flowing," "fresh," "full," "honest," "immediate," "loud but not too loud," "mellow," "natural," "not boomy," "not mushy," "not shrill," "not too cool," "not too dry," "precise," "pure," "realistic," "resonant," "responsive," "reverberant but not too reverberant," "rich," "singing," "smooth," "solid," "strong," "true," "vital," "warm," "wonderful"—seemed to be missing from his vocabulary. If Harris wants to praise a hall's acoustics, his highest encomium is "It has an exciting sound." Beyond that, one has to guess how much he likes it by the enthusi-

asm in his voice. If he is asked, he admits that he
regards Krannert, Kennedy, and Orchestra Hall as
"exciting," but it is difficult to persuade him to go
much beyond that; his favorite way of explaining the
sound of his own halls is to say, "I think most people
enjoy what they hear there."

For years, Harris has been saying that an acoustical
consultant should try to design a concert hall not for
himself and his personal preferences but for what he
thinks audiences want to hear, and for what musicians
on the stage, with their conductor, need to hear to play
their best. In Harris's opinion, the kind of sound that
fulfills those requirements is a constant as old as the
modern orchestra. He does not believe that it has been
affected by high-fidelity equipment and the prevalence
of recorded music in the home. (He has noticed, however, that concertgoers' manners are worse than they
were before hi-fi; people forget they are not at home,
and talk out loud, right through the music.) In part,
Harris's reticence about describing an acoustical ideal
reflects a feeling that such descriptions are wasted
effort; statistically, he assumes, no sound can please all
of the people all of the time. Still, the acoustics of
Krannert, Kennedy, and Orchestra Hall are much
more alike than they are different, and it is not difficult
to deduce what Harris means by "exciting." To some
extent, all of the critics' adjectives apply. "Exciting"
means astonishingly live: reverberant and full at every
frequency; marked by great clarity; with an extraordinary dynamic range, from triple pianissimo to double
forte; balanced; and with a powerful bass.

December, 1975: The fifteenth version of the ceiling
looked good. For each of the sloping planes that had

started out as the sides of pyramids there was now a matching plane, sloping at about the same angle in the opposite direction. The planes appeared to be rectangular, but none of them actually were; they had been carefully drawn to avoid right angles, if only by a few degrees. As a result, no two flat surfaces were exactly parallel. This was because Harris did not want any sound to become trapped—to bounce back and forth between parallel surfaces, instead of scattering. Some of the planes were no more than three inches long, for short-wavelength diffusion; some were twelve feet long, for long-wavelength diffusion; and the pattern of slopes was such that sounds with wavelengths longer than twelve feet would be diffused by a cluster of slopes that formed an obstacle on a larger scale. The plaster was to be applied on a metal-lath framework. There would be three layers of plaster on the lower side of the lathwork, and, finally, a coat of antique-white paint. There would also be a layer of plaster on the top side of the ceiling—a technique known as "back-plastering." All in all, it would be, in its detailing, the most complicated ceiling in the world. Yet the three men hoped that only a bored concertgoer with time to study the complexity of the slopes would pay any attention to it. "He will notice that it is not a flat ceiling, but he won't be especially interested," Johnson predicted. "He'll think that it is just a rough ceiling, rather rippled."

The balcony fronts, which looked extremely simple in the drawings, had evolved through a series of proposals almost as labyrinthine as the ceiling's. Harris had wanted a convex shape, and in the end the decision had been to make the balcony fronts semicylindrical, the quintessence of convexity—twenty-foot-long, hollow half-logs of heavy plaster, covered with gold leaf. They were to be stepped, overlapping a few feet, as the side boxes, moving back from the proscenium to the rear of the auditorium, were also to be stepped. No great acoustical point had been involved in that overlapping, but aesthetically it had been a puzzle. Johnson and Burgee had made full-scale models of the facings in their shop, and had fiddled around with them until they felt that the overlapping log ends looked just as they should.

January, 1976: The drawings and the specifications were finished and had gone out for bids. Morse was assembling a large force of subcontractors who would work under his supervision, but just who would work would depend—all other things being equal—on how much money they wanted for their parts of the project. Most of the bidders had track records of their own; Morse could not take a chance on using, say, a company that had never panelled wooden side walls as elaborate, and as acoustics-dominated, as the side walls that Harris, Johnson, and Burgee had designed. Many of the subcontractors would therefore be Lincoln Center veterans—companies whose employees had worked on other buildings in the complex, including the original Philharmonic Hall.

The finished plans included a good deal of remodelling that was only indirectly connected with the new auditorium. Ames, Mazzola, Moseley, and Fisher had decided to take advantage of the fact that Avery Fisher Hall would be out of commission for five months to make a number of other improvements. (Lincoln Center, the Charles A. Dana and William Randolph Hearst Foundations, Carl Morse, and the

Philharmonic Society would share this expense.) For instance, concertgoers had always had to pick their way around the Philharmonic Café, the restaurant on the Plaza level, just inside the hall's front doors. The café had never made any money, so it would be eliminated, but not the bar just behind it. Eliminating the café would release space for a new box office, right inside the front doors, where strangers had always looked for it. (The old box office, most easily approached by entering the side doors, was hard to find.) There would also be room to maneuver between the front doors and the new box office, so that the ticket-takers could be repositioned and concertgoers could move more easily up the escalators and stairs to the auditorium level, one flight above. The musicians needed better locker rooms, better storage rooms for their instruments, and a better lounge, most of which would be located below the stage level. Visiting orchestras needed improved backstage facilities. The ceilings in the soundproof warmup rooms backstage were too low; in fact, a violinist could not play standing up for fear of stabbing the ceiling with the tip of his bow. In recent years, the number of women in the Philharmonic and all the other orchestras that played in the hall had increased by a good deal, and some arrangements had to be made for them. (Eliminating the old box office released some of the additional space required.) The fresh-air intake for the ventilation system was at the north, or Sixty-fifth Street, end of the building, only a few feet above the crosstown-bus stop, where M-29 buses often stood pouring diesel fumes out of their exhaust pipes. The air intake would be moved to the roof. The coat-checking rooms were so small that it took some time for the audience

to get their coats back after a concert. These rooms
would be enlarged, and the coatchecking system improved, to Harris's delight.

Before the end of the month, most of the bids had
come in, and Morse was able to tell Ames, Mazzola,
Moseley, and Fisher approximately what it would all
come to—provided that nothing in the drawings or
specifications was changed during the process of construction. The bids for the auditorium added up to
four million dollars, or half a million over the preliminary estimate. The other changes, backstage and in
the public areas, would come to a million more, making the total cost five million. (By the time the work
had been completed in October, the numbers had
risen to four million eight hundred and eighty-four
thousand for the auditorium and a million four hundred and ninety-nine thousand for the other areas, or
a total of six million three hundred and eighty-three
thousand.)

April, 1976: As the Philharmonic's hundred-and-
thirty-fourth season approached its end, O'Keefe
called a press conference for the eighth—a little more
than a year after the rebuilding project was first announced. (Everything had been set for months, but
there were still tickets to be sold for concerts to be
given in the old hall, so it had seemed foolish to rush
to remind the public that the old hall's acoustics were
faulty.) The press conference took place at eleven-
fifteen in the Grand Promenade of Fisher Hall, beneath the two suspended sections of Richard Lippold's wire-and-metal-strip sculpture. The day was
sunny and beautiful. Chairs had been arranged class-
room style—ten rows of twelve chairs apiece, with an

aisle down the center—and about a third of them were occupied. Seated in a row facing the class—and with the Henry Moore sculpture in front of the Vivian Beaumont Theatre at their backs—were Ames, Mazzola, Fisher, Johnson, Harris, Moseley, and Burgee. Mazzola, who had been breakfasting at Gracie Mansion with Mayor Beame and was wearing a "Big Apple" pin on the lapel of his dark-blue pinstripe suit, was the master of ceremonies. He introduced Ames, who described how Harris, Johnson, and Burgee had been working as a "real team." It was hard not to have confidence in the results, Ames said. Mazzola introduced Harris, who almost immediately asked whether any of the reporters had questions. Hands shot up.

"You say that you know the new hall is going to work," one reporter said. "Can you absolutely guarantee that?"

There was a momentary pause, and a sprinkling of laughter from other reporters. Harris smiled a small smile. "Well," Harris said, "all the greatest concert halls in the world are rectangular—not that every rectangular hall is good." That drew a little laughter, too. "And then, I am using no new techniques or materials," Harris continued, "but only the things I have used in other halls, which are generally regarded as halls of excellence."

The questioner was not entirely satisfied.

"Can you *predict* how the new hall will sound?"

"I'd rather have you come and listen to a concert," Harris said.

"I'll come, but I am curious."

Harris nodded, acknowledging the fairness of the point. "I expect that it will have a full bass," he said, "and more uniform dispersion of sound throughout the hall, and that the audiences and the performers will be happier."

May, 1976: On Thursday the thirteenth, Harris seized his last chance to sit in on a Philharmonic rehearsal. Boulez was rehearsing Mahler's Seventh Symphony for the final concert of the season, on the Saturday evening two days later—the last concert in the old hall. By now, having attended practice sessions on an irregular schedule—sometimes two or three in a week, sometimes one in three weeks—Harris had met all the musicians, and he knew several of them fairly well. The sight of Harris walking onstage and slipping into an empty chair had become so familiar that the orchestra members scarcely noticed him.

Harris, Johnson, and Burgee had finished their design for the stage, so Harris was not seeking last-minute revelations about the orchestra's plight. The new stage floor would be of wood, like the old floor, but it would be mounted in quite a different fashion; it was to be constructed much like the floor of the new auditorium—oak on plywood on masonry supports, over an air space. Harris expected that the new floor would be more resonant than the old. The cellists and bass players should appreciate that, because part of the sound that their instruments make is transmitted through the floor via the tailpins on which they rest; ideally, these musicians should be able to play as loudly as the conductor wants without straining their bow arms. There would be four ascending wooden risers, or platforms, at the rear of the stage for the brasses, the woodwinds, and the percussion. Seen from the audience, the brown oak walls and ceiling of the stage would form a receding series of diminishing rectangles, repeating the shape of the proscenium and faintly reminiscent of the inside of the bellows of an old-fashioned portrait-view camera; the rectangular rear wall of the stage would be about half as big as the proscenium's opening. The orchestra would be playing in an enclosure like a shell, and it was designed to reflect some sound into the auditorium and some right back to the orchestra—in delicate balance, adding to the powerful throw of sound from the stage and, at the same time, ending the musicians' complaints that they could not hear each other play. Harris had discovered, by the way, that at times the orchestra had had trouble seeing as well as hearing. He had been sitting with the flutes at an afternoon rehearsal some months earlier when somebody left the auditorium by a door at the back of the balcony. A shaft of blinding sunlight hit Harris in the face. "You know, that happens all the time when we give an afternoon performance," the principal flutist, Julius Baker, said. "Someone goes out on a bright afternoon, and we are blinded for several seconds. It is impossible to follow the score." In the new hall, there would be curtains seven feet beyond each of the doors at the rear of the hall. Unless the doors and the curtains are opened simultaneously, which is not likely while the orchestra is playing, the sun would not shine in.

Harris had made a special point of attending the last rehearsal, because he wanted to make a ten-second speech to the musicians. The first break in the rehearsal, which had started at ten-fifteen in the morning, was at noon. When it was over, Harris, instead of Boulez, came out of the wings and mounted the podium. The orchestra, surprised, laughed and then applauded.

"I just wanted to thank you for all your hospitality all these months," Harris said. "You have helped me, and I hope in the fall you are going to think that I have helped you."

On Saturday night, the concert ended at 10:42 P.M., and before eleven o'clock stagehands had begun to unfasten the auditorium seats and move them out into the lobbies. Meanwhile, Harris and his wife joined Mazzola, Moseley, and Boulez backstage. Boulez was wearing a construction worker's white hard hat, which Moseley had presented him for his final bow. He looked good in it—jaunty. Several of the musicians came up and told Harris that they would be happy to help with the demolition if he would give them sledge-hammers. But there was no party or other ceremony to mark the occasion, which was, if not unhappy, bittersweet. The old hall had been the first out-and-out concert hall built in New York City since 1891, when Carnegie Hall was finished. It was less than fourteen years old, and it was about to be demolished.

If Harris has a secret unknown to other acoustical consultants (he insists that he does not), it lies in the importance he attaches to what he calls "field inspection." From the moment construction starts, Harris begins to visit the site, in order to make sure that the workmen are doing the job described in the architect's blueprints and specifications. He starts out by making a visit every week or ten days, and the pace of his inspections gradually increases. The chances are that by the time a hall is close to completion he will be dropping in daily. Since Harris is not a consulting firm but a college professor who does consulting, he has no one to help him. He has no assistant, no staff—not even a secretary. (He does have a telephone-answering machine, and he occasionally hires typists and editorial assistants for specific tasks, mostly in connection with his work as a writer and editor.) In any case, it would be difficult for him to find an assistant to do field inspection. Harris sees construction work with trained eyes. He would have to find someone else who not only knew acoustics but had watched a lot of concert halls being built. Even so, Harris probably would not trust an assistant completely. Contractors may substitute cheaper materials, not imagining that the acoustics of the hall could be affected. Workmen may do sloppy work, not thinking about anything at all. Or, worse, workmen may decide to do a more elaborate job than the plans call for, believing that some oddity in the design must be an error. (Air-conditioning contractors, for instance, apparently thought they were helping by straightening out odd angles and turns in ducts, which Harris had designed that way in order to reduce noise.) No matter how meticulously plans have been drawn, unforeseen problems arise, and Harris likes to have a part in solving them, just to make sure that the acoustics won't suffer.

On Saturday, May 29th—just two weeks after the final concert—Harris made his third inspection trip. Demolition was in full swing but had a long way to go, and yet the construction work had already begun: the man in charge of the ornamental-plaster work, Amerigo Catani, had started to cast the semicylindrical balcony and box facings. The whole interior of the hall was filled with pipe scaffolding, creating the world's largest jungle gym. Workmen with pneumatic jackhammers had knocked down most of the two old ceilings and were nibbling at the side walls and the balconies. The racket was deafening; there was not only the jackhammers' noise but the crash of falling chunks of plaster and concrete. Catani had created a plaster-casting shop for himself, at some remove from the racket, on the third-tier promenade, toward the Sixty-fifth Street end of the building. He had so far cast half a dozen heavy plaster shells, using a semicircular horizontal mold, and had fitted a skeleton of curved metal rods and braces into the interior of two of them. He had taken these two down three flights in one of the big freight elevators, and, in a workshop in the basement, had set them up on sawhorses in simulated balcony-front position. On Harris's instructions, given the day before, Catani had tied the metal framework of rods and braces in place with long lengths of wood fibres that resembled hemp. Then he had back-plastered everything in place, covering the ties with rough lumps of plaster and, in effect, bonding the framework and the shell together, so that nothing was loose to rattle or buzz and each section had considerable rigidity.

Harris was stopping by to inspect the two samples, which, if Harris approved them, would serve as models for a hundred or more that Catani still had to make. Harris and Catani had worked together before—on the balcony facings for the Metropolitan Opera House, in 1966. Each man had considerable regard for the other's competence. Harris looked closely at the internal structure of the section. "Is the plaster dry?" he asked.

"It's fairly dry," Catani said.

Harris took hold of the framework and tried to jiggle it. It was rock solid. Catani's attention was fixed on Harris's every move. Catani is in his early sixties (there are no youthful ornamental plasterers), with an olive complexion and a deeply lined, impressive face. He is short and thickset and, in a slow-moving fashion, agile.

"I had some trouble getting this plaster," Catani said. "They don't carry enough of it in the builders' supply houses. Nobody uses plaster of this grade except dentists and sculptors."

"It looks better than it did yesterday," Harris said.

"It is better," Catani said. "You know, this material for the ties is costing me a hundred and eighty dollars a bale. Can you believe that?"

Harris agreed that the price was steep. "I don't see why it should be that expensive," he said. "Isn't there something simpler you could use—some old-fashioned material?"

Catani shook his head. "This *is* the old-fashioned material," he said.

Harris walked around the castings and began slapping their convex surfaces with the flat palm of his hand. He slapped them all over, from right to left and back. He slapped their upper sides and he slapped their lower sides. The facings were like dead drums, and each slap was a dull thunk. However, the thunks varied considerably in pitch, and that was just what Harris wanted. Although the balcony facings, being convex, would make for good diffusion, they would also, like everything else in the hall, absorb a little sound. They would absorb some at all wavelengths, but how much low-frequency absorption there would be, compared to the middle- and high-frequency absorption, would depend in large measure on their resonances.

"That sounds good," Harris said. "But I notice that on both of these you've mounted the center rod of the

framework exactly in the middle of the casting. I wonder if you couldn't offset that an inch or so?"

Catani looked thoughtful. "Well, sure," he said.
"That wouldn't cost us anything."

"I'd like them all to be a little different," Harris said.
"Make one an inch off-center this way, and the next an
inch that way. Or two inches. Keep varying the place-
ment. Because"—Harris slapped the plaster twice—
"the more variety we get in that sound the better."

Catani nodded. "You're the boss," he said. "That's
just how we'll do it."

July, 1976: Five months is a short time in which to
demolish one auditorium and build another, and by
the middle of July two-fifths of the time was gone.
More than nine thousand tons of concrete, plaster,
and wood had been painstakingly carted out of the
building in dump trucks that were self-propelled but
had to be steered by hand—after they had been loaded
by hand—mostly up wooden ramps that had been laid
on the remnants of the old floor, through gaping holes
in the rear wall of the auditorium, where doors had
once been, across the east end of the Grand Promenade, and out through the space left after four of the
towering glass windows facing east had been removed.
(They were scheduled for replacement in October.)
There the debris had been dumped into a wooden
chute, where it slid down into trailer bins parked in the
taxi-access road and subsequently hauled away. There
were many more tons to go, because the demolition
was far from complete. At the same time, new materials were arriving—bags of plaster and cement, concrete blocks, steel rods and girders—and were being
stored in all the public areas except that part of the

third-tier promenade where Catani had his workshop. Water and air hoses and electric cables snaked around over the floors and into the auditorium—or the cavern where the auditorium had been. Everything—including the leaves of the big rubber trees in round cement pots in the Grand Promenade—was covered with a whitish film of plaster dust. Nearly four hundred workmen were on the job. A few were at work at almost any time of day or night, but most of them arrived at eight in the morning and worked until four in the afternoon, like construction workers on any job. Their superintendent was Ernest Benzoni—known to everyone as Ernie—who represented the Morse/Diesel Construction Corporation. His command post was a long, narrow room in the basement, outfitted with a desk, three chairs, a couple of four-drawer file cabinets, and a telephone, and was brilliantly lit by bare fluorescent tubes on the ceiling. Along most of one long wall was a shelf, slanted like an artist's or draftsman's drawing board. On it, in mild disorder, were all the drawings for the new hall, ready for quick reference. Benzoni had the book of specifications broken down into sections—mechanical systems, masonry, plastering, and so on—with each section in its own loose-leaf binder. In one corner of the room, under a table, there was a rack with nine niches for the kind of walkie-talkie radios that the New York City policemen carry. Benzoni communicated with his subordinates all over the building by radio, and the crackling and squawking of the instruments were almost as nerve-racking as the noise of the jackhammers.

Harris stopped by in the afternoon of Friday the twenty-third, on his way home from Columbia, signed himself in (a "Visitors' Register" was kept at the stage

door, on Sixty-fifth Street, which had become the main
entrance during construction), and walked quickly
through a maze of corridors and outer rooms to Benzoni's sanctum. It was Harris's tenth visit to the site
since the end of May.

"Good afternoon, Dr. Harris," Benzoni said, with
faintly mocking formality. Benzoni is tall, deeply sun-
tanned, and extremely handsome. He looks like an
American hero—like the Minuteman statue at Con-
cord, in fact. He moves like an athlete.

"Hi, Ernie," Harris said. Harris was wearing a
checked madras sports jacket, and now he took it off
and hung it up on a hook on the wall. "Got any problems?"

"I've got nothing but problems," Benzoni said. It is
true that from a foreman's point of view construction-
site problems come so fast all day long that they over-
lap, but what Benzoni meant was that he did not have
any serious problems.

However, Benzoni *was* concerned about the mount-
ings for the side-wall wooden panels. The concrete-
block walls were going up fast, and it would soon be
time to start fitting some of the prefabricated panelling in place. Harris and Benzoni conferred about this
for five or ten minutes and decided to mount two
panels, experimentally, in two slightly different ways.
Harris could decide which way was preferable, perhaps on his next inspection.

Benzoni moved to the shelf with the blueprints on
it and opened up the sheaf of drawings to one that
showed the ceiling design in great detail. Harris stood
beside him. Benzoni tapped the drawing with his pencil. "I've been studying this ceiling," he said. "Who in
the world ever dreamed this thing up?"

"Oh, that's architecture," Harris said. "The architects and I sort of batted the thing back and forth."

"I looked at the plans, and I said forget it. It can't be done. It can't be built. But slowly, the more I looked at it, I began to see some sense to it," Benzoni said. Benzoni was not serious. His story was elaborate hyperbole—a form of construction-foreman humor. He understood the ceiling perfectly, and, in fact, had invented an ingenious large-scale template, which fitted flat against the lathwork and showed the workmen the precise angle of pitch for each of the ceiling's planes. "Has there ever been a ceiling this complicated?" Benzoni asked.

"Well, the Minneapolis ceiling is pretty complicated," Harris said.

"But this one is more complicated, isn't it?"

Harris nodded.

Benzoni looked enormously pleased. "Well, I've got news for you," he said. "One whole section of it is up, and the scratch plaster is already on." (Scratch plaster is a rough coat, incised with closely spaced lines to give the second coat a surface it can adhere to.)

Harris's eyes opened wide. He had been waiting impatiently to see the actual ceiling begin to take form. He quickly opened a file drawer in which he kept his white hard hat, put the hat on, rushed to the freight elevators, rode to the top floor, climbed a ladder, and walked out on the temporary wooden flooring on the scaffolding's topmost level. If one looked down between the planks, the distance to the floor was fifty feet —five stories—but Harris has spent so much time on scaffolding and on catwalks between roofs and ceilings that he has learned to ignore heights.

The plastered section of the lathwork was still wet.

It was a soft gray and smelled like bread dough. Compared to the thousands of square feet still to go (the metalworkers had assembled only part of the lathwork for the ceiling), the plastered section was small—perhaps fifteen feet wide and thirty feet long. Still, the much discussed planes had emerged in their very bold relief, the distance from the top of the deepest indentation to the lowest angular extension being about two feet.

Harris examined the ceiling carefully. In some spots, the plaster was too thin, but on the whole the work looked good to him. After a few minutes, Harris went back down to Benzoni's office to compliment him.

Benzoni was already aware of the thin spots, and assured Harris that they would be fixed. "After it's finished," Benzoni said, "I believe you could show this ceiling to any builder, and tell him, 'Make me one like this,' and he would never be able to do it. I just hope it works. This ceiling may be my specialty for the rest of my life. I may go on making this same ceiling again and again, all over the world, until I retire."

August, 1976: Harris was on vacation. He was spending the first three weeks of August in a rented house at Truro, near the tip of Cape Cod. He had not forgotten Avery Fisher Hall, but his wife had persuaded him that some time away from work in the course of the year was good common sense. Harris agreed—he loves fishing and clamming—provided he could make a quick trip to New York every week or ten days to make sure that all was going well at Lincoln Center.

On Wednesday the eleventh, at 7:57 A.M., Harris

was in Benzoni's office. (He had lost half a day's time on account of Hurricane Belle.)

"I thought you were on vacation," Benzoni said.

"This *is* my vacation," Harris replied. He asked Benzoni how he was feeling.

"My head is filled with the work," Benzoni said. "I think of nothing except getting the work out. Please do not ask me if we are on schedule. I imagine that we *are* on schedule, but who knows?"

The ideal completion date, as of August, was October 10th, and everyone hoped it would not be much later than October 15th, so that the orchestra would have a few days to get ready for the opening concert, on the evening of Tuesday, October 19th—Boulez conducting the Brahms Concerto for Violin and Orchestra, with Nathan Milstein as the soloist, and the 1910 version of Stravinsky's "The Firebird." In that case, the evening before, the orchestra would play a special workmen's concert—a sort of preview to which all those who had worked on the project would be invited. But if for any reason completion was delayed, the regular subscription season, which was due to start on October 21st, might begin at the Beacon Theatre, an old movie house at Broadway and Seventy-fourth Street, where the acoustics are not a bit bad, despite a large balcony overhang, because its designer took delight in coffered ceilings, chandeliers, ornamental plastering, and statues. In *that* case, the opening concert would be postponed to an indefinite future day, and Harris would be greatly disappointed, for he wanted the orchestra to have as much rehearsal time in the new hall as possible before it, and the new acoustics, went on full public display together. The Philharmonic musicians, of course, are highly professional, and the orchestra can be flown anywhere in the world and play well in auditoriums it has never heard of, much less played in. Nevertheless, Harris thought that the orchestra should have time to adjust to the liveliness of the new Avery Fisher Hall—the more time the better. Harris draws an analogy, with qualifications, between concert halls and musical instruments. "No matter how good a violinist you are," he points out, "you cannot get the full tone out of a Stradivarius when playing it for the first time."

"I'd like you to take another look at the wall panels," Benzoni said. "And we've got a couple of the balcony facings in place, and we may be running into a little problem there."

Harris hung his jacket—this one of faded blue linen —on a hook, and put on his hard hat. Benzoni was accompanying Harris on this inspection, along with several other supervisors: a man from Morse/Diesel; Tom Bellingham, of Johnson/Burgee; and one of Benzoni's assistant foremen. The group moved toward the freight elevators. The corridors were crowded with hard-hatted construction workers waiting to be lifted to the levels where their work was. They were mostly young and big, and were full of conversation, mostly teasing. They wore fancy sports shirts and T-shirts. One youthful behemoth, weighing at least two hundred and twenty-five pounds, was wearing a T-shirt bearing the words "Long Island Little League." As Benzoni, who was leading the group, with Harris right behind him, approached, the construction workers moved aside, in deference to the boss. Catani was standing at the elevators, looking worried. He told Benzoni that he had hired an additional ornamental plasterer, who had been expected to report that morning but had not shown up. Benzoni took his walkie-talkie off his belt, pushed a button, and blew into the microphone. The radio squawked back, with an accompanying crackle of static.

"Have you got somebody in front looking for Mr. Catani?" Benzoni asked.

The answer was unintelligible.

"Mr. Catani, the ornamental plasterer," Benzoni added.

Squeals from the radio.

"They've got him," Benzoni said. "They're sending him back."

Catani looked greatly relieved. "He's a good man," Catani said. "And I couldn't find him until yesterday."

The scaffolding was still in place, but from the rear of the third-tier balcony, where Harris and the group entered the auditorium, it was possible to perceive a hint of the finished hall—the long straight lines of the stepped boxes, a piece of the ceiling, the fronts of the balconies. Things were much quieter than they had been, because demolition was over and the jackhammers had stopped. The machinery that was now in use —mechanical concrete surfacers, compressors to pump ceiling plaster from the Plaza level to the top of the scaffolding—was merely noisy.

The specifications said that the prefabricated wooden panels could not be considered properly attached until they had been "impact tested." In practice, the impact test consisted of Harris's hitting them, sometimes with the palm of his hand, sometimes with his fist, in much the same way he had slapped the balcony facings. Fitting the panels had been a problem, because the concrete-block walls were not perfectly plumb-line straight. Adjust-

ments had been made in the vertical wooden strips,
known as grounds, that were nailed to the blocks,
and in the thickness of the compressed fibre glass
between the panels and the walls. Harris eased his
way along the side-box underpinnings to a place
where several panels had been mounted. While everybody—and especially the carpenter who had
done the mounting, the day before—watched rather
apprehensively, Harris slapped and pounded and
listened. Then he started up a ladder, reached out,
and slapped higher up. "Yes," Harris said. "I think
that's going to be all right."

The group moved on to the box where two of
Catani's castings were in place, fitted against the front
edge of the floor. Catani and his new assistant were
waiting. Catani looked a little uneasy. Harris knelt
down, reached over, and slapped the convex surface.
He tried to wiggle the mounting brackets with his
fingers, but they did not move. Benzoni casually
stepped off the ledge he was standing on, thirty-five
feet in the air, hooked an arm around one of the scaf-
fold's pipes, and stood on a rod two inches wide in
midair so that he could get a better view of the pro-
ceedings. Harris shifted his position, and hit the facing
from a slightly different angle. He stood up straight.

"No," Harris said. "That isn't going to work. We
will have to get some more plaster in there." Harris
conferred with Benzoni. Benzoni talked to Catani.
Catani's new assistant looked bewildered. Harris
talked to Benzoni some more.

Benzoni, who had been frowning, was finally convinced. "Oh, sure," he said. "We can get some plaster
in there all right. And we'll do it."

September, 1976: Early on Monday the thirteenth, Harris dropped off corrected page proofs of his "Historic Architecture Sourcebook" at McGraw-Hill's offices, at Sixth Avenue and Forty-ninth Street, and took the subway to Lincoln Center. He got his hard hat from Benzoni's office, and in a matter of minutes he was examining the wooden floor of the hall. For the past two weeks, Harris had been visiting the site almost daily. Half the scaffolding had been removed— the half farthest from the stage—since the ceiling there had been given its final coat of antique-white paint. Nearly all the plywood underflooring was in place; it had been laid around the pipe feet of the scaffolding while the scaffolding was up, leaving small round holes to be plugged after the scaffolding came down. Carpenters were at work laying the oak floor. Starting from the back, they had completed almost a quarter of the total area. The boards, of random lengths and only two and a half inches wide, ran across the hall from side to side. The wood was white oak, which was to be stained dark brown. All but two sections of the balcony facings were mounted. Across the three balcony fronts, where the facings were not stepped but ran in straight horizontals for nearly seventy feet, they made a bold chalk-white pattern. Many of the rows of small lights beneath the front edges of the balconies and boxes were in place and had been turned on to test the wiring before the fixtures were completed. For the first time since May, the auditorium was brightly lit.

With one month left, much of the work still to be done was on the stage and in the area immediately surrounding it. Most of the dark-oak wall panels were in place, covered with temporary protective fibre

board and plastic sheeting. (Plaster dust might dis-
color them; an accidental blow—say, by a piece of pipe
as the scaffolding was dismantled—could make a dent
that would be hard to repair.) But the carpenters were
just starting on the oak floor and risers on the stage,
and its front wall had not been built. Harris examined
the rear and side stage panels closely, and slapped
several of them with his fist. They sounded solid.

All summer, Morse had reported to Ames at inter-
vals on the progress of the work—always optimisti-
cally. Now the Philharmonic needed to be told with
certainty whether the opening concert could be held
on the evening of Tuesday, October 19th. Shortly
after eleven o'clock, Morse, who had been inspecting
the hall since before nine o'clock, promised that the
work would be finished no later than the eighteenth—
in time to allow the orchestra to give the workmen's
concert that evening. This was encouraging but Harris
hoped that Morse could do even better. In Harris's
opinion, a week of rehearsals in the new hall, getting
used to the new acoustics, would not be a bit too
much.

During Harris's mid-September field inspections,
while the finishers—plasterers, carpenters, painters,
electricians, air-conditioning installers—were swarm-
ing over the site, one of the questions in the forefront
of his mind concerned the hall's dynamic range. He
hoped it would be extraordinarily wide, so that the
contrast between pianissimo and fortissimo would be
dazzling. For the quiet end of the spread, Harris had
inherited a building with good insulation against outside noises—trucks, airplanes, helicopters, subway
trains. He had improved upon this protection by the

fortresslike construction of the new auditorium's walls, ceiling, and floors. As for inside noises, the old air-conditioning presented problems. The ducts had all been replaced, and were all lined with sound-absorbing material; there were flexible connection joints, resilient hangers, sound traps, and sound barriers. The velocity of the air in the system was to be low, in order to keep it from making an audible whoosh as it entered the hall through slots in the ceiling and grilles above the balconies and boxes. Air-conditioning systems are rated for noise on a special decibel scale—the Noise Criterion Scale. Harris aimed for a level no higher than NC-20, at which the air-conditioning would pass for noiseless, because two thousand seven hundred and forty-two people, even at their most rapt, make about that much noise, and one sound would mask the other. Harris was alert for any sign that a ventilation duct had been damaged (a bent metal flange might whistle) or had been carelessly installed (a duct touching a pipe might rattle). If everything went right, the audience would be able to hear a chair scraped on the stage floor, and if a trumpet player dropped his mouthpiece the noise would be audible in the last seat of the top tier.

While insulation against outside noise sets the low end of a hall's dynamic range, a sum of positive qualities—not merely the absence of noise—determines the high end. The orchestra should be able to produce a spine-tingling fortissimo of tremendous power—an impossibility in a dead hall, no matter how much physical energy the musicians put into their bowing, blowing, beating, and so on. Given an equal effort on the musician's part, an instrument sounds louder in a live hall with plenty of diffusion than in a dead hall. If the

audience hears the correct proportions of direct and
reflected sound, the orchestra can be at once loud and
musical—especially if earlier pianissimos have been
marvellously delicate. A forte can be well balanced,
with all sections taking their proper part, all instruments in character (the clarinets sounding like clarinets, the cellos like cellos, and so on), and each choir
clear and finely detailed, without great exertion by any
section. (As Harris had come to know the Philharmonic musicians, one after another had expressed the
same wish: that his instrument could be heard without
his having to "force." That was not mere laziness, for
forcing distorts an instrument's harmonics and spoils
its natural timbre.)

Harris has often described a good hall as a "tight"
hall, meaning one in which a minimum amount of
sound escapes through cracks or holes before the audience has had a chance to savor the music fully—a
flaw that Harris calls "wasting sound," or "throwing
sound away." Sounds die their natural deaths by absorption soon enough; there is no sense in letting
them out into spaces above the ceiling or into the
promenade areas or into the basement, where they
would be of use to no one. So Harris was concerned
that all the doors were sound-tight when they were
closed. They were heavy metal doors, to begin with,
certified as "soundproof" and gasketed. When they
were properly hung, they sealed themselves against
sound leakage at their tops and sides as they closed,
and, as they latched, a sealing device at the bottom of
the door moved down a quarter of an inch, closing off
the crack at the bottom. The ceiling light fixtures were
another possible avenue for escaping sound. They
were designed so that each row could be lowered on

cables—like a circus trapeze—to the orchestra floor if a bulb needed changing or a socket had to be repaired. When one of the trapezes was raised and in place, however, it nestled into a sound-seal: above the first seal there was a second seal, and above the second a third. That seemed enough to discourage almost any errant sound. Harris checked to see that this triple-defense system fitted as had been planned. The air-conditioning vents also needed attention. Much of the incoming air was to enter through great ceiling slots —each four inches wide and about eighty feet long. Inevitably, some sound would escape through these apertures, but in order to minimize the loss the ceiling slots were shielded from the orchestra by plaster beams; a certain amount of reflected sound would get away, but the direct sound would bounce off the beams before it reached the slots. All the air went out through holes in the floor the size of dinner plates. Most of them were covered with raised fittings that resembled mushroom caps, which would reflect some sound while the stale air passed under their raised edges. The mushroom caps were under the seats, which would be under the patrons. Sound loss through the floor would be minimal.

By September 20th, almost all the flooring had been laid in the body of the hall, and about a third of it had been stained dark brown. All the scaffolding was down, but only temporarily; the schedule called for some of it to be reërected for work on the stage ceiling and the balcony fronts. Carpenters were finishing the front stage riser. There were workmen on all three balcony tiers, pursuing their specialties. To meet the deadline, less than a month away, they were following each other as quickly as possible. Plasterers were plastering the ceiling above the second balcony while, just a few feet away, painters were rolling a final coat of antique-white paint on the wall panelling behind the second tier of boxes. Some of the gold seats had arrived, in a giant trailer truck, which was parked on Sixty-fifth Street. Their installation was to begin, starting at the rear of the orchestra, either that night or the following morning.

Harris had been escorting a friend around the site. They stood on the stage and looked out to the back of the hall. "You can really begin to see it," Harris said. "Almost as if it were finished. But there's a tremendous amount of work yet to be done. Not quite a month to go. If this were an ordinary construction job, you would say they needed another three months."

October, 1976: With two and a half weeks remaining, Lincoln Center, Inc., was maintaining an official air of quiet confidence in the forthcoming acoustics, but the suspense was high. Ames, Mazzola, Moseley, and Fisher were refraining from predictions, and even the Philharmonic's flyer for the 1976–77 subscription season, which had already been mailed, refrained from premature boasting. It mentioned the fact that the concerts would be presented in a *new* Avery Fisher Hall, but it left prospective subscribers some leeway to guess what "new" might mean:

For 134 consecutive years the Philharmonic has been sharing musical adventures with the greatest city in the world and we want you to join us for our 135th season.

A new hall has been created for our outstanding orchestra and with subscription seats you will guarantee your place among the thousands who share the joy of the Philharmonic experience.

As Mazzola had explained to an interviewer early in the summer, during the demolition phase of the work, the public-relations strategy was "to stick to the substance." Mazzola, personifying assurance, had said, "When we are ready to open, *we* are certainly not going to say, 'The sound will be great.' All we are going to say is 'Come and listen.' The acoustics will have to sell themselves."

Harris was cheerful. That might have been taken as an affirmative clue, except that Harris had seemed cheerful even when he was worried. Twenty-one months earlier, he had promised Lincoln Center a hall of excellence, and it was evident that he had no thought of wasting time by repeating himself. On Saturday, October 2nd, Harris stopped in for his daily visit at about noon. Compared to earlier Saturdays, the auditorium was quiet. No more than two dozen men were at work, and some of them were sprucing up the public areas outside the hall proper: painters in the Grand Promenade, on mechanical ladders, were changing the fifty-foot columns and the fronts of the three overhanging promenades to dark brown from their previous cream and dark green, and a crew of workmen was cleaning the steps by scattering bright-green sawdust on them and then sweeping it up. The Lippold sculpture had been dusted, frond by frond. Sections of plate glass that had been removed for debris disposal were back in place. Inside the auditorium, carpenters were working on the two rear stage risers, and electricians were tinkering with the lights in the stage ceiling. Other electricians were fitting long

brass strips underneath the facings of the balconies
and the side boxes—the visible part of the fixtures
that, all told, were to hold more than five hundred
light bulbs, which would outline the bottom edges of
all three tiers. Painters were getting the balcony and
the proscenium and the forward edges of the sections
of the orchestra shell ready for their gold leaf—putting on a coat of yellow-brown filler, then spackling
wherever the surface was not perfectly smooth, and
putting on a second coat of filler. The gold leaf was
not supposed to be applied until all work with power
saws had been finished and the hall had been cleaned
thoroughly, because dust in the air or on the surfaces
to be covered could spoil the process. Ernie Benzoni
hoped that the gold-leafers could start by that Monday
at the latest.

Harris was eager to test the noisiness of the air-
conditioning system as soon as possible. If the "silence" exceeded NC-20 for any seat location anywhere in the house, and if the trouble could not be
repaired in time, the opening concert might have to be
postponed. On Wednesday, October 6th, the system
was ready to be turned on for the first time. Harris
came down from Columbia late in the afternoon, carrying his sound-level meter in its black leather case.
He had understood that all the workmen would be
finished for the day at five o'clock, which would have
suited him—even the quietest work, or a whisper,
would spoil his measurements. To his disappointment, there had been a last-minute change. A dozen
workmen—two gold-leafers, four seat-installers, four
painters, and a pair of electricians—were still at work,
and they planned to continue for several hours.

The new air-conditioning has seven component systems, each with its own blower, designated AC-1 through AC-7. AC-1, which ventilates the stage, could not be turned on, because the gold-leafers were working in that area. A rush of air, a change in temperature, or a change in humidity might damage the gold leaf they had just applied. Harris did what he could. He had the man in the control room in the basement turn circuits AC-2 through AC-7 to full power. At Harris's request, an assistant foreman announced a surprise ten-minute coffee break for all hands. Harris, accompanied by Ray Kallberg, who represented Syska & Hennessy, the mechanical engineers for the hall, took a few preliminary readings in the orchestra and some in the top tier of the balcony. Harris's meter was the size and shape of a carton of extra-long cigarettes, with a narrow extension at one end housing its microphone. He balanced the meter against his belt, pointed the microphone toward the nearest air outlet, manipulated the dials, and read out series of numbers in a calm but concerned tone of voice. As Harris read, Kallberg plotted the numbers on a piece of paper with the NC-20 curve marked on it. Harris's meter, an octave-band analyzer, divides sound into eight frequency ranges, each an octave wide, and each designated by its middle frequency—62.5, 125, 250, 500, 1000, 2000, 4000, and 8000 cycles per second. To ordinary ears, the noise in the hall was nonexistent, except when, from time to time, the workmen whispered and were immediately asked to keep quiet. To Harris's meter, and to Harris's ears, however, and according to the X marks Kallberg entered on his chart, the air-conditioning was a little too noisy in the higher octave bands—something like NC-25, instead of

NC-20. "The good thing," Harris said, "is that we seem to be all right in the low frequencies. If we were getting too much noise at sixty-two point five or one-twenty-five, that could be really big trouble—maybe with the fans or in the ducts. But of course I'll have to come back and take a complete set of measurements when we can turn on AC-1, too. And I hope we will be able to locate the problem in the higher frequencies."

That was easier said than done. The finishers were again working around the clock, hoping that the hall —the stage, in particular—would be near enough completion for orchestra rehearsals on Wednesday the thirteenth and Thursday the fourteenth. Harris needed at least a full half hour of silence to test the noise level with all circuits operating. Much as he hated to delay the other work, he arranged for a half-hour intermission from midnight on the twelfth to twelve-thirty on the morning of the thirteenth. "All right, quiet everybody!" shouted an assistant foreman. "You're on, Dr. Harris, and this is costing about a thousand dollars a minute."

Ernie Benzoni, who had been working since eight o'clock in the morning, followed Harris and Kallberg around the stage as Harris took several readings. AC-1 was a little noisy. AC-5 and AC-6, the two circuits that air-condition the executive offices, had not seemed troublesome before, but now were adding to the noise. (Harris's meter could detect the difference when AC-5 and AC-6 were shut down completely, leaving the rest on full.) All in all, the noise level on the stage was only slightly above NC-20, but it was enough above it to upset Harris. He decided, nonetheless, that the rehearsal should go ahead, as tentatively scheduled. At 12:45 A.M.—a few minutes later than planned—the workmen were back on their jobs.

Before he went home that night, Harris discovered part of the explanation for the stage noise.

The walls of the dimmer room on the third floor, where some electrical controls are located, were not completely finished. Benzoni thought they could be finished before 10 A.M., when the rehearsal was to start. Then, to make sure that the orchestra wouldn't be distressed, AC-5 and AC-6 could be kept turned off until the rehearsal was over. "What's important," Harris told Benzoni, "is to turn the air-conditioning on a couple of hours ahead of time, and then to keep the humidity just as constant as you can."

Wednesday's rehearsals went well. The orchestra seemed happy, even though the new locker rooms were still a mess and the music was interrupted from time to time by banging and hammering. Harris was at the hall all day and well into the evening, trying to track down the noises. Thursday's rehearsals went better. Harris was greatly pleased by the number of compliments he got from orchestra members. At 10 P.M. on Friday the fifteenth, Harris retested the air-conditioning noise. The completed walls in the dimmer room had been covered with sound-absorptive board, but the return air system for AC-1 was still making a slight noise. At a little past midnight, Harris crawled into a space beneath the stage and decided that a bent turning-vane inside one of the air ducts, at a rounded bend, must be causing the trouble. The turning-vane was not absolutely essential, and if it was causing the noise it would be better to get rid of it. On Saturday morning, October 16th, a workman opened up the duct. He removed the turning-vane and saw, to his surprise, a clutter of rubble—bits of cement or plaster that had fallen into the air passageway. That small pile of debris had been constricting the flow of air, increasing its velocity, and creating a noisy turbulence. It was cleaned out. Sound-absorptive material was added to the duct. By late that afternoon, AC–1 was fixed. With all the air-conditioning turned on, the noise level at all seat locations was no higher than NC–20. No one would be able to hear a thing.

By the afternoon of Monday, October 18th, the orchestra had rehearsed in Avery Fisher Hall four times, and Harris was elated by the musicians' response. There were bound to be some, he assumed, who did not like the new hall, but he had not heard any complaints. He had attended all the rehearsals, and dozens of the musicians had made a point of thanking him. They had all mentioned how well they could hear themselves and the other sections. One of the double-bass players had talked about being able to *feel* his instrument producing, and he had meant "feel" it with his toes. The principal horn player, John Cerminaro, was delighted with not having to force. "I think you've added twenty years to my professional life," he said. Avery Fisher, who had been listening since the first rehearsal, said that the first sound of the strings tuning up was all he had needed. Moseley was tremendously pleased, and so were Ames and Mazzola. Boulez felt that the clarity of the sound was a delight.

Harris's spirits were high and he was also tired. He had practically lived at Avery Fisher Hall for the past week, and had stayed long past midnight on three occasions. Harris had heard what he most wanted to hear: the sound, which was extraordinarily clear, died away evenly, bespeaking a decay curve of admirable smoothness, and justifying all his efforts to endow the auditorium with plenty of diffusion.

Later on Monday afternoon, Harris sat in his apartment, waiting to be interviewed by Irving Lowens, the music critic for the Washington *Star*. Had it not been for that appointment, Harris would have taken a nap, to be fresh for the preliminary concert that night in honor of the construction workers. As it was, he sat chatting with a friend. "You know something?" Harris said. "That Philip Johnson is an amazing architect. I should say Johnson and Burgee, because they are a real partnership. I have been over every inch of that place with them, time and time again, for the better part of two years. We've talked and talked, and thrashed over the drawings. But I didn't really *see* everything they were doing until just these past few days. What a marvellous place to give a concert!"

A plan to exclude critics and reporters from the workmen's concert had collapsed, under pressure, some days earlier. Instead, the Philharmonic was welcoming the press but requesting that nothing be written about the acoustics until after the gala opening concert the following night, October 19th. At least an hour before starting time, which was eight-thirty, most of the capacity audience—construction workers, their wives and children, music critics, newspaper reporters, architectural critics, contractors, subcontractors, managers, agents, musical celebrities, Lincoln Center brass hats, and the orchestra's guarantors, sponsors, and patrons who could not stand the suspense for another twenty-four hours—were in the building, exploring the new hall. They looked much like an ordinary Philharmonic audience—that is to say, well-dressed—but their prevailing mood was giggly, like that of high-school seniors at their graduation exer-

cises. Ames, Fisher, Moseley, Johnson, Burgee, Mazzola, and their parties were in the first-tier side boxes,
near the stage. (Harris's plan was to move around and
listen from a variety of places.) They looked cheerful.
While the orchestra was waiting for Boulez to make his
entrance, several of the musicians spotted friends or
relatives in the audience, and waved to them. Boulez
appeared, and *he* looked cheerful, too. The house qui-
eted. Just before Boulez raised his arms to conduct
"The Star-Spangled Banner," one of the second vio-
lins scraped his chair, ever so slightly. He got a reprov-
ing look from a violist, not far away.

The program consisted of the second and fourth
movements of Mahler's Symphony No. 9 and excerpts
from "The Firebird." Some time after the concert was
over, Dr. and Mrs. Harris and Mr. and Mrs. Ames were
still standing in the Grand Promenade, accepting con-
gratulations and saying good night, as if they were
hosts at a party—as was the case. Their faces showed
their own pleasure. Ames seemed a trifle reserved
about expressing his opinion, as if he feared that he
might be accused of having tried to influence others'
judgments. However, he was responding with great
warmth to the nice things that were being said to him
about the sound of the hall. Someone said to Ames
that the pianissimo at the end of the Mahler had been
remarkable for its delicacy and beauty. "Indeed so,"
Ames said, beaming. "Remarkable. I don't believe I
have ever heard a pianissimo quite like that anywhere
else in the world."

\*

As far as *The New Yorker* was concerned, the crucial
verdict on the new acoustics was the opinion of its own
music critic, Andrew Porter, and he had expressed his

first reactions in his column, "Musical Events," in the November 1 issue, the week before my account of the rebuilding appeared. Porter had liked what he had heard. ("The new Avery Fisher Hall is a success," Porter declared, and he explained in some detail why he was giving his "unqualified initial approval for the acoustics.") Critics from all over the world came to inspect and judge, and, with only a dissonant note or two, they liked what they heard. The new hall drew an unbelievable amount of attention in newspapers and magazines in almost every country. O'Keefe told me afterwards that, in column inches, nothing that had ever happened at Lincoln Center had been assigned more space. Since the suspense was really over before my article appeared, I loved Harris's reaction to it. He called me up. "I read it through last night," he said, "and it made me nervous. I really began to worry whether everything would work out."

Avery Fisher is undoubtedly a concert hall of excellence, and Harris has pretty well convinced me that I should not waste my own time wondering whether it is the best in the world. Even so, I wonder. I am practically certain that it is. Still, knowing how much Harris hears that I don't hear, although my hearing is good, I would like to have Harris confirm my belief. He will not do so, I know. Were I to press him to name his favorite concert hall, it would not be Avery Fisher, or the Great Hall in Champaign-Urbana, or the Concert Hall at Kennedy, or Orchestra Hall in Minneapolis, but the new hall he is working on for the Church of the Later-Day Saints in Salt Lake City, Utah, where the concrete foundations have just been poured.